W9-BBH-640

CONTENTS

INTRODUCTION

What does the word 'archeology' conjure up in your mind? If you are like most people, it undoubtedly evokes images of great ruined temples and cities: Machu Picchu, Zimbabwe, Angkor Wat, the great structures of the Nile Valley, the Mayan ceremonial centers and many others. This is understandable, for such remains naturally excite the imagination; it is easy to see why the layman tends to believe that archeology deals mainly with monuments of this kind.

And, to be sure, archeologists have dug and reconstructed these buried temples and lost cities, just as they have unearthed golden treasures and royal dead. This book describes its share of such spectacular finds. But there is far more to the story of archeology today, something intrinsically more stimulating and potentially more significant than just the 'umpteenth' retelling of the 'exciting' story of how these obviously impressive remains were discovered and excavated. It is this more modern—and we feel, more

Examples of the traditional 'glamorous' conception of archeology are such sites as (above) a Mayan ceremonial center in Central America and (right) Machu Picchu in Peru.

4

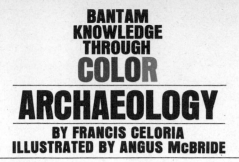

BANTAM KNOWLEDGE THROUGH COLOR

ARCHAEOLOGY

BY FRANCIS CELORIA
ILLUSTRATED BY ANGUS McBRIDE

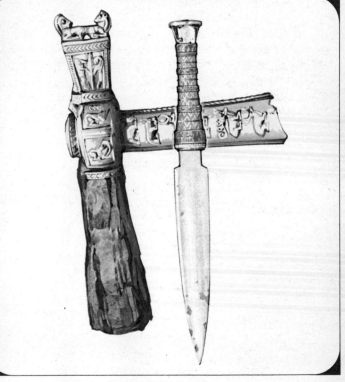

BANTAM BOOKS
TORONTO   NEW YORK   LONDON

FOREWORD

The search for our history and past—the focus of archaeology—is a subject hard to rival in interest. Hundreds of
amateurs and professionals have hunted and dug in lands
all over the globe, putting together the remains of man's
glories and failures, day-to-day living and grandiose enter-
prise over the course of his existence. In ARCHAE-
OLOGY, Dr. Francis Celoria, an acknowledged expert
in the field, provides a concise account of an unusually
vast subject. Beginning with early man's diversified stone
cultures, Dr. Celoria traces man's development through
the great civilizations of the Near East, Greece and Rome.
A unique section of the book concerns itself with the
methods and practices of archaeology: prospecting for
sites, conducting "digs," surveying and recording and the
conservation and restoration of artifacts. The text is com-
plemented by 450 full-color illustrations.

RLI: VLM 10 (VLR 10-11)
      ─────────────────────
      IL 9-adult

ARCHAEOLOGY

*A Bantam Book/published by arrangement with
Grosset & Dunlap, Inc.*

PRINTING HISTORY
*Grosset & Dunlap All-Color Guide hardcover edition
published August 1973
Bantam edition published July 1974*

*Bantam Books are published by Bantam Books, Inc. Its trade-
mark, consisting of the words "Bantam Books" and the por-
trayal of a bantam, is registered in the United States Patent
Office and in other countries. Marca Registrada. Bantam
Books, Inc., 666 Fifth Avenue, New York, New York 10019.*

PRINTED IN THE UNITED STATES OF AMERICA

exciting—version of archeology that this book presents. It is a story as up-to-date as radiocarbon dating, magnetometers, scuba-diving, aerial photography, and all the other advanced techniques that have forced archeological research to move as fast as any discipline and forced archeologists to reassess continuously the pieces that make up the great jigsaw puzzle of man's past.

Perhaps we can best approach what this book is about if we consider the word 'archeology' again. It is derived from two Greek words meaning 'ancient' and 'study': archeology thus seeks to recreate the story of man's past, specifically through studying his material remains or traces, although when written records have survived archeologists naturally make use of them, too. At times, archeologists must work in a library or study or laboratory, studying what has previously been found or thought and then synthesizing this in some coherent form—usually an article or book.

But behind all archeology lies active fieldwork—'digging' —although this does not always involve moving masses of dirt, anymore than it always produces spectacular finds. Archeologists spend most of their time dealing with what is left of the day-to-day belongings of very ordinary people. Working with every bit of evidence, the archeologist attempts to put together a picture of a part of the past—the way primitive men lived thousands of years ago in caves, or the way civilized men lived in ancient Athens.

Operating as both an art and a science, archeology can

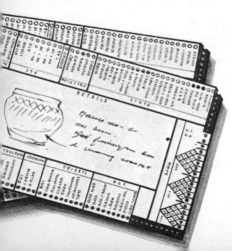

Typical of modern archeological techniques are these cards prepared for computer classification and analysis of a culture's pottery.

bring its special techniques to bear on any period. The earliest stone tools made by men are obvious material for the archeologist's skills, but so is a nineteenth-century watermill; there is no rigid time limit for archeology. The main criterion is: will the archeologist be the best person to sort out the story of a particular site or period?

There are several ways to present the results of archeologists' work. Our approach is to relate their discoveries in the form of a continuous reconstruction of mankind's own history rather than as the story of individual archeologists and their 'digs'. Space does not permit a description of every single culture or site—thus, there is no mention of the Khazars or the Picts or the Olmecs—but the reader is given a selection that should provide a sense of general patterns and developments. It will be possible to see what preceded what and to grasp the often strange back-and-forth fluctuations in the complex and dynamic story of man in the past.

Limitations of space have also required us to restrict our coverage, so that we have chosen to concentrate on the earlier and lesser-known stages of man's culture, tapering off about the time that classic civilizations began to employ writing. It is these earlier stages that archeologists have done so much to help reconstruct and in which so many of the more recent and crucial breakthroughs have been made. And rather than describe large-scale excavations, we shall be showing the way archeologists grapple with the facts they have discovered. This is the truly exciting side of archeology, this constant and continuing search, and it seems far better, when learning the elements of archeology, to face up to the incompleteness of man's story and to see how provisional are many archeological reconstructions.

A word should be said about archeologists. Some of the famous early archeologists, such as the German Heinrich Schliemann or the Englishman General Pitt Rivers, made a vigorous entry into the subject rather late in their careers. Others, like the Dane C. J. Thomsen or the Australian V. G. Childe, were more gentle scholars who had pioneering minds ideal for new interpretations. Some, such as the

Some famous archeologists: (left) Pitt Rivers; (center) Schiemann; (right) Breuil.

French priest Henri Breuil, Pei-Wen-Chung from China, the Briton L. S. B. Leakey, or the American Carl Blegen, have mingled energy in the field with profundity in the study. More and more, the ideal archeologist is asked to be scholar, teacher, organizer and, above all, a leader—as exemplified by the American Robert Braidwood or the Briton Sir Mortimer Wheeler—but even the many archeologists who work unobtrusively must possess some of the same spark that has fired the more famous pioneers and thinkers.

Even though modern archeology is very much a subject for experts, one that requires a disciplined training, this does not mean that the amateur cannot share in the study of man's past. He may even be able to contribute to that knowledge, not so much by digging as by careful observation and speedy reporting of any chance finds—and many finds are still being made by non-professionals, whether it is a young boy discovering a cave or a worker bulldozing for a foundation site. This book's final aim, indeed, is to educate the beginner's eye so that he might learn to recognize remains of the past. And who knows, perhaps someday you might add a small piece to the great puzzle that is modern archeology.

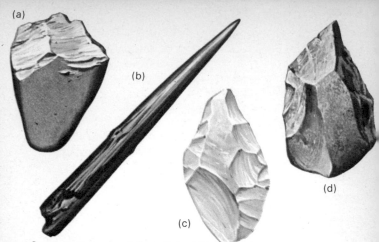

Some basic types of Early Paleolithic tools: (a) pebble tool; (b) yew spearhead; (c) and (d) handaxes

THE PALEOLITHIC OR OLD STONE AGE

Relics of people who lived literally hundreds of thousands of years ago have been found in Europe, Africa and Asia. Observers have picked up many tools made of flint and other available stone in gravel beds, river deposits and even, in Africa, lying on the ground. The most common tools are oval or pointed axelike objects called handaxes. We are still not certain how they were used; they were probably general-purpose tools for grubbing, hacking and, possibly, cleaning skins.

It is because such simple stone tools, along with a few remains of human skulls and skeletons, are all that have survived from the first period of human culture that we call it the Paleolithic, or Old Stone, Age. Until fairly recently, this period was thought to go back a million or so years, but more recent finds indicate that man may have been making simple tools for more like two or even three million years. Before man made handaxes, incidentally, he used split or roughly pointed pebbles that would be almost unrecognizable as man-made were it not for their being found in considerable quantities in contexts suggesting the presence of man.

Besides the chunky handaxe, less shapely chopping tools and choppers have been found. In addition, early man also used flakes of stone, sometimes adroitly struck. Some early items need an experienced eye to recognize, but later developments show that a large piece of stone was carefully prepared so that one tap with something heavy could produce a sharp flake with strong cutting or scraping edges arranged as the toolmaker wanted.

Occasional evidence of wooden spearheads has been discovered, and in Africa and elsewhere there are finds that have led archeologists to suggest that wood and antler tools were used. Most of the non-stone tools of Paleolithic man have perished, as have the majority of his physical remains.

In China and Africa, sites have been found where fire was used, so Paleolithic man probably knew how to cook some foods. Some of the animals he saw were similar to those of today, but many, such as the mammoth, have long been extinct. Beyond this, we do not know much about the culture of these hunter-gatherers. Paradoxically, we know more about the extremes of cold they survived in the Ice Age and of the warm conditions that punctuated retreats of the ice.

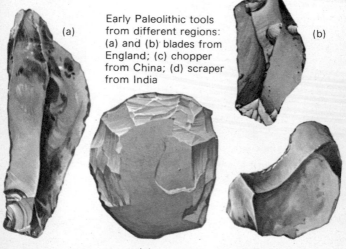

Early Paleolithic tools from different regions: (a) and (b) blades from England; (c) chopper from China; (d) scraper from India

(a)

(b)

(c)

(d)

Paleolithic Man's Environment

Most people have heard of the 'Ice Age' but they have only vague notions of its date, duration, or extent. The layman may be forgiven some confusion, for each decade of research has forced the specialists to change certain ideas of the Ice Age. For instance, earlier estimates were that it began 600,000 years ago, but this period is now considered to have lasted perhaps three times as long, starting about 1½ million years ago. And man's status and environment at the start of the Ice Age is still problematic.

When we refer to the Ice Age we are speaking of the one that fell in the period the geologists call the Pleistocene—millions of years before there had been other ice ages. During the Pleistocene, the great sheets of ice advanced and retreated several times, and between *glaciations* came periods of considerable warmth known as *interglacials*. The number of major glaciations varied in different regions of the world—North America and northern Europe seem to have experi-

Typical Ice Age deposits: I, interglacial; II, glacial. Symbols indicate tool finds.

enced four—and the ice by no means covered the whole world, but one thing was constant: these fluctuations had tremendous effect on the climate of the world and thereby on the environment in which early man was developing. When the ice sheets in the Northern Hemisphere were in their final retreat—say, between about 12,000 to 8,000 B.C. —man was very much a product of his many adaptations to this changing environment, not only in his physical body but also in whatever culture he had developed.

How do we measure and identify this period during which man as we know him came on the scene? Geologists, as we said, know it as the Pleistocene Period and they have a number of 'gauges' with which they map the time sequence —evidence of cold and warm periods is one, the distinctive animal fossils, which range from mammoths to small rodents, is another. Another key to the chronology of the Pleistocene is provided by the layers of different types of soil, such as gravels or the wind-blown loess deposits. And deep borings in the Atlantic and Pacific have also produced detailed evidence of past climatic history.

But after the geologists and other scientists have cooperated to fix the sequence and duration of the various parts of the Ice Age, the archeologist must fit man into the picture. Perhaps the greatest difficulty in dating Pleistocene deposits containing man or his tools is encountered in areas far from the two poles—areas such as the Sahara Desert. In such areas, the geologists have not found deposits that reflect glacial or interglacial conditions. Accordingly, geologists have postulated the existence of rainy or *pluvial* periods to correspond with glacial periods, with *interpluvials* corresponding to interglacials. Evidence of pluvials and interpluvials has helped date some human deposits, but the investigations are far from error-free.

The glacial and interglacial periods, as is expected, affected the levels of the oceans and seas as well as rivers and lakes connected with them. Often an 'ancient shoreline' well inland today has furnished a clue to a Paleolithic settlement. On the other hand, it should be remembered that in parts of the world, some previously occupied areas are now under water.

Lower Paleolithic in Europe, Asia and Africa

Half a million years before the end of the Ice Age, Paleolithic man in the Old World evidently possessed the three
basic means that would take him still farther from his pri-
mate relatives: fire, speech, and stone tools. But while the
next few hundred thousand years may not have witnessed
any comparable cultural developments, men did make a
variety of stone tools. They are now named from the places
where they were first recorded, and the beginner should
at least be aware of these technical terms.

The earliest *pebble-tools* to merit systematic study have
been named *Oldowan* from the African finding place. Later
came man's first standardized tool, the handaxe; the earlier,
rougher ones are called *Abbevillian*, and the later, more
elegant ones, *Acheulian*. Man probably used stone flakes
quite early; two examples of the earliest noted in local con-
centrations are the thick *Clactonian* flakes and the early
Punjabi flakes. Later man became more skillful in remov-
ing thick flakes from stone cores in a planned pattern. The
technique, usually named after finds of the *Levallois* culture
in France, was an impressive one.

Areas where handaxes have been found

Area of cultures without handaxes

Although handaxes were made in a vast arc from southern Africa to India, the Far East tended to make its own variants of Paleolithic tools. In China at Chou K'ou Tien, rough *choppers* and *chopping-tools* and flakes, rather than handaxes of the Acheulian type, were made by Peking Man. In the Indian subcontinent we find examples of the *Soan* choppers (cores flaked or sharpened on one side of an edge) and chopping tools (cores flaked on both sides of the cutting edge).

Central and southern Africa developed local variants of the Paleolithic cultures. The *Sangoan*, which existed nearer the time of the last glaciation in Europe, and definitely after the African Acheulian, was a jungle culture with picks, lanceheads and a broad-edged ax. Another post-Acheulian culture was the *Fauresmith*, which had flakes as well as core tools and has been found from Kenya to South Africa.

Each excavation season produces more far-flung examples of early Paleolithic cultures. Crude Paleolithic tools have turned up in Japan, and doubtless others will be found in other parts of the world.

An artist's 'reconstruction' of Neanderthal Man

Neanderthal Man

About 100,000 years ago there appeared a man now known as Neanderthal (after the site in Germany where his remains were first recorded). Although best known from French and European excavations, his bones and distinctive stone tools have also been found in North Africa and in the Near and Middle East. He lived largely in the cold world of the final glaciation, but the conditions were often far from arctic. Then, between 40,000 and 30,000 years ago, Neanderthal Man seems to have disappeared, but it is not certain whether he was killed off, pushed into inhospitable areas where he died out, or 'merged' into modern man.

Early flint tools

Neanderthal Man was a skilled maker of flint tools. He made handaxes not unlike those of the earlier Acheulian culture; he knew the Levallois technique of striking sharp, shaped flakes from a carefully prepared core of flint. His later tool kit contained some flint 'blades' which are distinctive of the Upper, or Advanced, Paleolithic Age, near the end of the Ice Age, when men more like ourselves dominated the scene.

Neanderthal Man types go back many thousands of years, though we have information on only the last phases. Often Neanderthal Man buried his dead in specially dug graves, occasionally covering the burial with a slab. Meat was left in some graves (for an afterlife?). Sometimes a 'magical' red ochreous powder was sprinkled over the corpse.

Much speculation has gone into Neanderthal Man's way of life or culture, which is named the 'Mousterian' culture from an important site called Le Moustier, in France. But it is the origin of this kind of man which causes most discussion. Scientists are currently describing ourselves as *Homo sapiens sapiens*, and Neanderthal Man as *Homo sapiens neanderthalensis*. Thus we no longer claim him as a separate species. Some hundreds of thousands of years ago there appeared on the scene an earlier version of ourselves which, while remaining within the definition of *Homo sapiens*, evolved into the Neanderthal man in question. In other words, there was an early stock of *Homo sapiens* which probably developed into Neanderthal Man and similar types (called neanderthaloids) in certain areas, while also giving rise to modern *Homo sapiens* in other places. But specialists hesitate to announce any complete conclusions when the total finds of early man would barely fill a small truck.

Mousterian burial

15

Upper Paleolithic: Europe, Asia, Africa

For hundreds of thousands of years, man made handaxes or produced broad flakes of flint and other stone. Then, in the last glaciation, *Homo sapiens* as we know him today entered Europe. While many specialists have argued that *Homo sapiens* moved westward into Europe, it is still uncertain where he originated. But certain facts stand out clearly. He had art and was already widespread enough to have many varieties of culture. From about 40,000 to 10,000 B.C., in the last Ice Age, there developed cultures, especially in southwestern France, which clearly show that it was in western Europe that the Advanced, or Upper, Paleolithic had its finest manifestations. Although Upper Paleolithic sites and remains have been found in western Asia and in Africa, and more and more art of that period is being discovered outside western Europe, the sites in France offer most to an investigator.

Besides art, Upper Paleolithic cultures offer two new

Advanced Paleolithic implements: left, from Africa; right, from Siberia

Advanced Paleolithic points: left, from United States; right, from eastern Europe

features: the use of many bone and antler pointed tools, and the manufacture of bladelike flakes that were blanks for making specialized implements for groove-cutting or scraping. Techniques or implements used in later periods were anticipated: the making of baked clay objects; geometrically shaped small implements that were to be so common in the Middle Stone Age; the building of shelters and structures in the open, which were more complex than mere lean-tos.

Like the Neanderthals, Upper Paleolithic Man buried his dead. Only now the bodies were flexed (knees to chest), as well as being sprinkled with red ocher. Women were buried with their necklaces and jewelry (made of shells, or animal teeth, or an occasional fossil), together with their babies.

Man by now was no savage who instantly attacked other groups. We assume this from the fact that men at the end of the Paleolithic could obtain shells from a sea miles away or bring hematite (a red iron ore) hundreds of miles to color beads.

17

Upper Paleolithic Tools

Although occasional blades of flint were made into points and knives in the times when Acheulian handaxes were made or when Mousterian flakes were struck by Neanderthal Man, it was not until some 40,000 years ago that man appears to have acquired a passion for making blade tools. In any blade-making culture we find the fluted or prismatic cores from which blades have been struck. They vary in dimension from nut-sized to the so-called 'Gigantolith' cores of the Ukraine—a foot long—possibly tools in their own right.

Sometimes the blades were blunted on one edge, just like our steel jackknives. Some blades were struck so that the edge planes intersected to provide a sturdy engraving edge; this was the burin or graver. Often a blade was delicately trimmed by careful flaking to make an endscraper.

Some flints were flaked skillfully until the parallel scars produced flutings side by side (making one end like the cowcatcher of an old locomotive). This is called a plane. Certain cultures of the Upper Paleolithic, such as the Solutrean, made exceptionally thin leaf-shaped spearheads or knives.

Burins were the tools used to draw outlines of animal shapes or to carve or decorate bone objects. These blade-derived tools were used to make a distinctive implement, the bone or reindeer antler point. Needles of bone also became common in the later part of the Upper Paleolithic. Another characteristic piece of Advanced Paleolithic equipment was the spear thrower, used as an extension of the arm.

By the end of the 1960s it became possible to assemble a broad view of the Upper Paleolithic from Wales to Japan. This period which ranges, according to current estimates, from 40,000 B.C. to about 10,000 B.C. offers a variety of cultures that show how complex man's life was then. Even without the evidence of skillfully made tools or of Ice Age art, we would still be impressed by the traces of huts or tent bases found in the U.S.S.R., France and elsewhere.

A Paleolithic shell neckl

	Years Ago	
Neolithic	7,000	**Neolithic** Agriculture Metalworking
Magdalenian	15,000	**Mesolithic**
Solutrean Perigordian Aurignacian	40,000	**Late Paleolithic**
Mousterian Levalloisian	160,000	**Middle Paleolithic**
Acheulean Chellean Abbevillian Oldowan	500,000 to 1,500,000	**Early Paleolithic**

Generalized chart showing the major divisions of the 'Stone Age' in the Old World. It is to be remembered that the time divisions are somewhat arbitrary and that geographically separated cultures progressed at varying rates. This applies especially to the Mesolithic, which is very much a transitional period.

The Spread of Upper Paleolithic Cultures

In studying the last glaciation in Asia and Europe it is possible to discern at many sites the contrast, with some overlaps, between the sequence of Mousterian flakes and the blades of Upper Paleolithic man. In an inter-stadial, or warm, phase of the last glaciation there may have arisen just the right conditions for modern man to develop new techniques or ways of life. Already in Hungary, Austria, Poland, Rumania, the Ukraine and elsewhere a culture called the *Szeletian*— which is post-Mousterian — was producing leaf-shaped spearheads or points with a new technique. Then, over 30,000 years ago appeared more certainly modern *Homo sapiens* with his blades and bone points. He did not originate in western Europe and we are still not certain where he came from. Guesses that it was from Palestine or beyond the Caucasus are of little help.

In France, where Upper Paleolithic cultures are richest, various workers have distinguished a *Perigordian* stage with blunted-back blades and points, some burins, and some broad flakes like Mousterian scrapers.

Following this there is the *Aurignacian* culture, which is

Artist's reconstruction of a Paleolithic tent

Burials are sometimes the only evidence we have of prehistoric culture

largely independent of the Perigordian. Aurignacian tool kits include split-base spear points of bone, endscrapers, chunky burins and nosed scrapers made from half a pebble. Implements of similar types have often been found in Asia and elsewhere but the label 'Aurignacian' has often been too freely conferred.

In France and elsewhere there then intruded a culture called the *Solutrean* with its characteristic leaf-shaped points which, like bone needles, supplemented a normal Upper Paleolithic equipment.

Next there arose the richest and most varied of the European cultures of the Upper Paleolithic, the *Magdalenian*. It is best known for its harpoons with twin runs of curved barbs, and a great variety of stone implements—many of them displaying great skill in producing a vast system of burins, tanged points and tiny borers—and quite a few small items that are precursors of the small flints or microliths of the post-glacial

Paleolithic flints and beads from Eastern Europe and central Asia

Middle Stone Age, or Mesolithic, period.

The Magdalenian is largely a western European culture, but parallels are found as far as Siberia. Similar cultures do not occur in, say, China or India; and often there seems a gap between the chunkier Lower Paleolithic items and the tiny microliths of the Mesolithic. But not every part of the world has been archeologically explored.

Some Late Paleolithic Cultures Outside Europe

In Africa there is no Upper Paleolithic tradition like those of the Aurignacian or Magdalenian of Europe. But in northwestern Africa and Kenya, *Homo sapiens* of the Capsian culture made stone blades and burins, together with small flints belonging more in style to the late Mesolithic. Moreover, the Capsian (c. 6000 B.C.) and an earlier culture beginning about 10,000 B.C. in Morocco, Spain and elsewhere—called the Iberomaurusian and noted for its tiny blades and points—are of the very end of the Pleistocene, much later than the allegedly similar cultures of Europe. So in Africa one speaks of a Middle Stone Age that bridges the gap between the Paleolithic and Neolithic. Many African Middle Stone Age cultures persisted until quite late and some of them used pottery.

In India and China there is again a very poor display of cultures that might be considered a bridge between the Paleolithic and the flints of post-glacial hunting cultures. In several parts of India, blade industries or cultures have occasionally turned up. They are not very plentiful and they were followed by a rich variety of cultures employing small stone tools, numerous examples of which have been found in recent years.

In northern China, as at Sjara-osso-gol (in Suiyuan in the great curve of the Yellow River), remains of a culture have been found over 100 hundred feet below ground. The assemblage discovered has blades and burins plus tiny bladelets that would not be dissimilar to Magdalenian ones from Europe. The Sjara-osso-gol finds are of a warm phase of the last glaciation, but few archeologists would confidently date these items. There is an earlier stone industry from Shui-tung-kou, also in Suiyuan, where blades were found with tools looking like Mousterian flakes. A date between 50,000 and 10,000 B.C. is the best that can be given at the moment with our present state of knowledge.

In Siberia there is an odd variation of the familiar pattern. There is an Upper Paleolithic having many features in common with those of Europe: blades, female figurines, bone implements and the like. One interesting feature is the use of huts or pit houses; the Siberian Upper Paleolithic was sometimes sedentary. Later in the same period came an astonishing change: tools became crude and sometimes resembled the pebble tools of early man. In contrast, the antler and bone harpoons were developed and cultures came into being that have much in common with some Eskimo cultures.

The story of man's progress has had many zig-zags during the course of time. Archeology reminds us that there could be halts in progress at any stage.

The variety of Upper Paleolithic art can be seen in the treatment of both animals and man.

Upper Paleolithic Art

In the Upper Paleolithic Age, man made a cultural leap forward that still staggers us today. In this period, between roughly 30,000 and 8,000 B.C., he developed an art of great complexity and variety: paintings and engravings on cave walls, and sculpture in stone, clay, bone and antler. No simple explanation of the motives, both group and individual, of this art can be found.

The lively horses of Lascaux (France) and the powerful bulls of Altamira (Spain) are too well known to be described here. These are spectacular examples, but there is a great quantity of other art which is being studied in increasing detail. The whole phenomenon of Paleolithic art belongs to the last glaciation and stretches from Portugal to the U.S.S.R., and from England to Africa. Every year new discoveries are being made.

The drawings themselves tell of the animals that were seen, slain and eaten by Paleolithic Man: mammoths, elephants, horses, reindeer, salmon, rhinoceros, bison—enough

A horse as portrayed by Paleolithic Man

animals to fill a zoo. Life was not necessarily always harsh, but it is difficult to imagine a leisured class of artists indulging in 'art for art's sake'. In trying to understand Paleolithic art, it is foolish to apply 20th-century ideas about the motivation of art, whether they are derived from the sophisticated artists or from the so-called 'primitive' artist. There have been fashions in explaining the art of the Old Stone Age, and the archeologist must suspect any single explanation for any human phenomenon.

At first it was suggested that the art, which predominantly portrayed animals, was hunting magic. Man drew the animals he wanted to catch. This hunting-magic hypothesis has been criticized on the grounds that some of the strange animals shown in cave art are considered to be either inedible or imaginary. Another theory argued that the animals were totem animals. Primitive man does not disengage himself readily from nature. In addition, he can consider animals, trees, and stones to be animated as men are. This animism and the totemism, which links the identity of

25

A mammoth—Paleolithic art from the U.S.S.R.

the individual or the group with an animal or a plant, would lead to representations of the totem and to rituals connected with it. Unfortunately, recent analyses of the relative numbers of species portrayed have created difficulties for those who regard the totem as the main motif.

It is easy to suggest that cave art was not just decoration. Sometimes drawings were in inaccessible recesses of caves. It is reasonable to suppose that in some cases the drawings could have been for 'initiation' ceremonies.

Another view is that the art is connected with fertility, whether of the animals to be hunted or of *Homo sapiens* himself. With growing confidence certain prehistorians have been relating more and more drawings and symbols to sex. There is something in this, but many illustrations such as those of a pensive mammoth or a defecating rhinoceros can hardly be described as sexual.

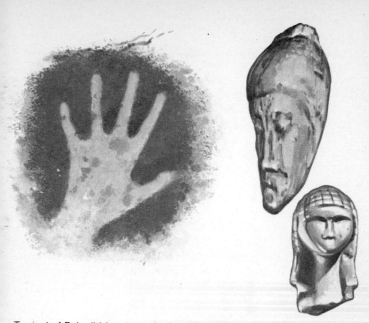

Typical of Paleolithic art are the hand impression and bone carvings.

While caution is needed, courage is required in visualizing possible explanations. Once it is realized that sometimes the art was created in the context of a mixture of personal and social motives and that the same kind of drawing was initiated at various times and places for completely different motives, then one can return to each painting or group of paintings with more understanding.

Paleolithic art used many techniques and media. There could be, for instance, engravings on rock, with or without color. Stone plaques found in one place bore designs of animals in a style found on cave walls miles away; hence the argument for a 'school' of artists. Lamps that lit the artists' work have been found, as well as shells full of ocher and other pigments. The paints were charcoal or simple minerals, mixed with water or fats. At some sites, evidence of blow-pipe-spraying of paint has been claimed.

The End of the Ice Age

Around 12,000–10,000 B.C., the ice that capped the Northern Hemisphere (as well as the Antarctic regions) began to retreat. The enormous quantities of water surged up as ice returned to the sea and the world's sea level rose. Areas such as Britain or Scandinavia, which had been under the weight of ice for thousands of years, began to rise out of the water and partly canceled the effect of the rising sea. Some land bridges were broken; others were uncovered. Australia and North America were possibly linked with Asia by open land around this time, although precise dates are difficult to produce.

The general climate of Europe and even its prevailing winds altered. Some animals adapted to warm climates while others, such as the mammoth or the reindeer, disappeared or moved north. Some men may have found this distressing and instead of basking in the warm weather moved north after the animals they knew so well. In French sites such as Mas d'Azil the barbed harpoons of reindeer antler were no longer to be found; instead red deer antler was used.

Perhaps the most significant change is in the vegetation. Archeologists and botanists have learned much from seeing in excavations the successive layers containing pollen and plant remains, beginning in the lower levels with the flora of a chilly, tundra-like environment not far from the ice-face. Plants like the dwarf-willow prevail at first, but slowly over eight thousand years each vegetation climax is reached and passed. There were times when the elm was more plentiful and flourishing in Europe than it is now; at other times, the climate was not so helpful. Besides fluctuations and climaxes there were several minor variations in the sea level such as the ones that flooded the fenlands, which are now the North Sea, or broke through to separate England from France.

Pollen survives astonishingly well over thousands of years. Left to right: pollen of oak, beech, pine, hazel, and birch trees.

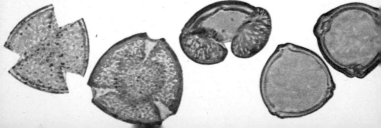

2,000 A.D.

BEECH AGE

Herbs
Heather
Birch (right)
Oak
Beech (left)

400 B.C.

OAK-ASH AGE

Oak (left)
Ash (right)
Birch
Hazel
Lime

2,500 B.C.

OAK-ELM AGE

Oak (left)
Elm (right)
Lime
Birch
Hazel

5,500 B.C.

PINE AGE

Birch
Scots Pine (left)
Hazel (right)
Common Alder

8,000 B.C.

TUNDRA AGE

Herbs
Dryas
Dwarf Birch (left)
Arctic Willow (right
Juniper

10,000 B.C.

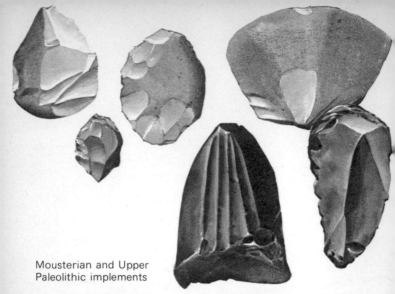

Mousterian and Upper
Paleolithic implements

The End of Paleolithic Cultures

In Europe there were many 'Mousterian' cultures which
were followed by Upper Paleolithic cultures. In the Near
East and North Africa the picture is complicated by the
presence near the end of the Pleistocene Ice Age of cultures
that are a hybrid of the Mousterian and the earlier Leval-
loisian 'flakes-from-prepared-cores' cultures—hence the be-
wildering term Levalloiso-Mousterian.

In Palestine, at Mount Carmel, blades (like Upper Paleolithic types) have been found in late Acheulian (handaxes)
deposits. Similarly, the roughly contemporary Levalloiso-
Mousterian flake-industries of the Near East and North
Africa have blades—and, more important, the human
remains resemble those of modern man. Here is the exciting nub of a great problem: when and where did modern
Homo sapiens develop? What was his culture and environment? Our answers to these questions are far from complete.
There have not been enough sites investigated, and it would
be naive to expect that the origins of Upper Paleolithic
Man will be found exclusively in the areas bounding the
southeastern coasts of the Mediterranean.

It is possible, as often is the case in archeology, that blade cultures developed out of Mousterian cultures independently. The Shanidar Cave (in Iraq), after being deserted by its Mousterian (Neanderthal) occupants, was left unoccupied for 10,000 years before the blade-makers came in. The reader should also be reminded at this point that it is only *assumed* that the makers of blades were modern *Homo sapiens;* many stone finds have no skeletons to go with them.

It may seem that too much space has been given here to the cultures of the tail-end of the Ice Age, but this is a necessary emphasis. Although it is easy for author and reader to gravitate to the more spectacular archeology of great civilizations where events and sequences are easier to grasp, the techniques of interpretations used for the Upper Paleolithic are the best training for the would-be archeologist. This kind of work is mentally tough and is more demanding than the archeology of other periods, since the prehistorian has to be an authority on the typology of implements and an expert on environment and skeletal finds.

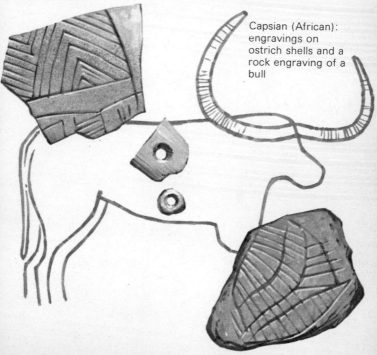

Capsian (African): engravings on ostrich shells and a rock engraving of a bull

TYPOLOGY

The person who is being introduced to archeology for the first time, and has read this far, may be a little restive by now. So many cultures, so many blade types, so many 'foreshadowings of the Mesolithic' and the like may make him feel that we have gone too far from people with hands, eyes, noses and ears, who grappled daily with their environment. But the archeologist must carry out inquiries as to the *dates* of things and their *origins* and *influences*. Dating by physical or chemical methods works only in certain circumstances, and the archeologist has often to rely on *typology:* This object is of a type usually found in the Upper Paleolithic. There being no other aspects of the context to cause doubts on the matter, we say that this object is of an Upper Paleolithic type, and therefore, of the Upper Paleolithic period. This is in many respects a very sensible thing to do. One can date an old car roughly, or sometimes quite accurately, because it is a 'pre-war type' or because it is a 'pre-1933 type', and so on. With cars, typology is all

The numbers indicate where the objects on the opposite page were found.

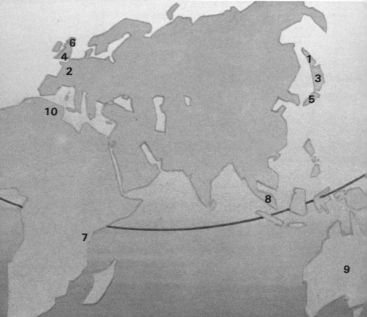

Typology can prove links, but it can mislead us with apparent similarities. Note where these similar types were found (on map opposite).

right, but man has archaizing tendencies, frequently introducing reproductions or imitations of 'vintage models'.

The flint blade, which is the 'typical' tool of the Upper Paleolithic of the last glaciation, was also made thousands of years before in the Acheulian. Blades were used thousands of years after the Paleolithic in the Neolithic, from Siberia to England. But the *frequency* of those blades not from the Upper Paleolithic is much less.

Similarly, an archeologist may find a flint flake made from a carefully prepared core, chipped so that if tapped at one point it would release a wide but thin flake which is just the shape the maker visualized. This technique is named the Levallois technique—after a place near Paris where these flakes (and their cores) were first recognized. The Levallois *culture* is thought to date to the glaciation before the last one, and to the warm interglacial period that preceded the last glaciation. But the technique also continued into the last glaciation in Europe, and longer elsewhere.

MAN IN THE AMERICAS

As far as we can tell, man first appeared in the Americas very much later than in other parts of the world. The general view is that he crossed the Bering Strait from Siberia to Alaska at a time when the sea was lower, or when there was an ice bridge. The migrants probably got across before the last glaciation ended.

Many American archeologists are prepared to accept the possibility that there were game-hunters where the United States is now even as early as 30,000 B.C., although most reliable radiocarbon datings from sites with implements still do not put the evidence much earlier than 20,000 B.C. There are many excavated examples of mammoth and other bones found with lancelike projectile points of stone, which are shouldered or fluted at the base. Most of these finds (from 13,000–5000 B.C.) are from the western United States and the plains, Mexico and parts of South America, though similar points are also found in the eastern states.

As the ice retreated and the climate grew drier and warmer, man learned to hunt different animals, such as the buffalo. There may also have been several new arrivals across the Bering Strait. By 5000 B.C., or even a few thousand years earlier, seed collection had become a major source of food, though hunting was certainly not neglected.

The cultivation of plants seems to have been developed at three or more centers. In Mexico and its borderlands, the squash and possibly other vegetables were already being cultivated by 6000 B.C. Beans and then corn followed between 5000 and 2000 B.C., perhaps preceded as a cereal by foxtail millet. A little later, root plants like manioc were cultivated in Venezuela, Peru and the Amazon area.

Pottery appeared before 2500 B.C. in both Central and South America, and by 1000 B.C. there were places in many parts of the continent that could be termed towns. All this was developed, as far as we know, without any contact with the Old World, though vigorous attempts are made periodically to show trans-Pacific linkages with the Far East.

Early clues of man in the Americas include the Folsom and Clovis stone tools of North America, animal skull of Middle America, and stone tools of South America.

Left: ax from France.
Right: various microliths.
Below: 'pick' from Spain.

MESOLITHIC CULTURES

The archeologist, faced by the complexity and variety of human cultures even ten or five thousand years ago, yearns to be able to label or classify his discoveries and then to make meaningful comparisons. The Paleolithic from the time of the handaxes to that of the Upper Paleolithic blades and harpoons is clear; so is the later Neolithic Age, with its polished axes. Before the 1880s, the contrast between the Paleolithic and the Neolithic was thought to be so obvious that archeologists postulated a Middle Stone Age, the Mesolithic, to explain certain finds.

Small flints—later called microliths—and waste items from their making, found in many parts of the world, came to be recognized as distinctive of the cultures that man adopted for hunting and food gathering after the ice had retreated around 10,000 B.C. The tundra, or woodland Mesolithic cultures of northern Europe and Asia, which had axes or picks as well as microliths, were well studied before 1914, but there was much uncertainty as to what Mesolithic cultures there were in more southern regions such as southwestern Asia or North Africa.

These questions are not irrelevant in discussions about man's cultural evolution, but they led to extreme distinctions, such as when there is no Mesolithic but a proto- or pre-Neolithic. Indeed, some of the key features of the Neolithic have occurred in Mesolithic cultures. To make matters more complex, cultures were found in northern Germany and elsewhere which looked too late to be Paleolithic and yet did not have enough Mesolithic features to be called Mesolithic.

Yet there are so many contrasts and overlaps between Paleolithic, Mesolithic and Neolithic cultures, especially in the Near East, that it would be naive to refuse to classify. Often, as with the proto-Neolithic Natufian (Palestine) or the earlier Neolithic of Shanidar (Iraq), it is possible to see some features in common with the Upper Paleolithic. In addition, the Natufian has offered evidence of sickles coated with the gloss obtained in cutting cereals.

It is becoming clearer that there are some areas that have not gone through the Mesolithic stage. In southern Africa a 'Late Stone Age' survived until the African Iron Age.

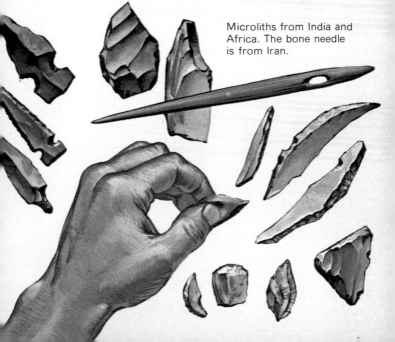

Microliths from India and Africa. The bone needle is from Iran.

Mesolithic Cultures of the North

As pointed out, the end of the Ice Age about 10,000 B.C. did not produce an abrupt change of equipment. Many Mesolithic cultures—such as the Azilian of France and Spain, and the northern European Ahrensburgian—have features in common with the Upper Paleolithic. The Azilian has barbed harpoons like those of the Magdalenian, but this time they are from the antlers of red deer, not reindeer. The mighty art of the Paleolithic is sometimes found surviving as reddish marks on pebbles. The Ahrensburgians, who lived (about 8500 B.C.) in tents all over the European plain, had—like the Polish Swiderian cultures of about 10,000 B.C. and later—blades and burins of Upper Paleolithic type and a few small microliths (small flints slotted into arrow or harpoon shafts to make barbs or 'teeth').

In the north of Europe, from the Baltic to Britain, there was an environment of trees, shrub-lands and marshes. It is not surprising that the people who

Top: Mesolithic carving from Yugoslavia. Center: Azilian painted pebbles. Bottom: stag-tooth necklace from Poland.

found a living hunting, catching fowl and gathering fruit used the bow and axes with broad cutting edges. At times there were axes of antler, and various experiments were tried in tool making. Sometimes flint axes were hafted in antler sleeves.

The Tardenoisian culture, noted in France and farther east, with its triangular and trapeze-like microliths, was already in touch with Neolithic folk. It was more advanced than the earlier Sauveterrian, with pointed flakes which have been found in Britain, France and elsewhere.

Another Mesolithic culture, whose dumps of shells in Denmark and Germany gave it its nickname of 'Kitchen-midden folk' was that of Ertebølle; a few pots found their way into their belongings.

Each region has its own post-glacial Mesolithic culture. For example, the coasts of Ireland, Scotland, Norway, Spain and Portugal produce rough stone tools which do not have microliths but are definitely Mesolithic in date.

Natufian flints and Danish bow and arrows

A northern Mesolithic settlement

Some Mesolithic Sites.

Star Carr

There is such a variety in the post-glacial sites that could be labeled as 'Mesolithic' that it will only be possible to select two well-studied excavations, each of which offers both extremes and overlaps. One is in England, at Star Carr in Yorkshire, where in the eighth millennium B.C. small groups of Mesolithic hunters and food-gatherers were squatters on a platform of birch stems by a reed-bordered lake.

The inhabitants settled at this spot sporadically, and only in late winter and early spring, but they seem to have had a good diet; they ate red and roe deer, elk, ox, pig, plant items such as the yellow water lily and bog beans.

Many small (microlithic) flint arrowheads were found and this is some evidence of the use of the bow. The other flint items ranged from burins and scrapers to an occasional flake ax. Red deer antler was used for making barbed harpoon points or fishing-fork prongs.

Among the items of special interest were a wood canoe paddle, fragments of birchbark containers, a pyrite fire-striker and fungus tinder. The life at Star Carr is regarded as being an early example of the Maglemosian culture that spread between the Baltic and western England.

The Belt Cave

The Belt Cave (or Ghar-i-Kamarband, the Cave of the Cummerbund) is by the shores of the Caspian in Iran, and is as far as possible from Star Carr in place and context. The excavators got down through to the base levels of this cave and of the nearby Hotu Cave. Near the bottom was an early Mesolithic site of around 9500 B.C., the time when the glaciations were coming to an end in the north. These Mesolithic people hunted seals with bow and arrow and, in addition, are thought to have had the dog as a domesticated animal. Around 6600 B.C. the people of this cave hunted a species of gazelle; a thousand years later they were Neolithic, bringing in pottery within a few hundred years.

Sites like Belt and Hotu never give a complete sequence from the Mesolithic to the full Neolithic, but they help produce a useful tentative picture.

Excavating in the Ghar-i-Kamarband cave in Iran

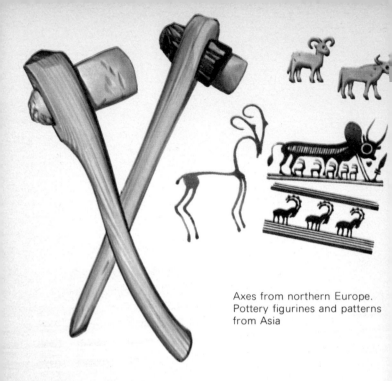

Axes from northern Europe. Pottery figurines and patterns from Asia

THE NEOLITHIC AGE

The word 'Neolithic', which refers to the 'New Stone' Age, has been in use for over 100 years. The word was originally used to label the polished stone axes that have been found in all the continents of the world. Later it was realized that the users of polished axes were also the first users of pots; eventually it was realized that Neolithic peoples were the first to domesticate animals and to cultivate plants. These last two features are the important ones, because stone tools seem to have been polished in both the Paleo-lithic and the Bronze Age.

The change to a Neolithic way of life was a startling one, since man changed from being a food-gatherer or a hunter to being a *food producer*. This means that instead of a large area (even 100 square miles or more) maintaining a few persons, a relatively small area of cultivated land and pasture could maintain hundreds of people. Of course, not all peoples became sedentary after the Neolithic.

While no one doubts the radical changes that the Neolithic brought into man's life, it was a gradual process rather than a sharp revolution. Pottery, domestic animals, cultivated plants and polished axes did not appear on the same day! In some areas, such as Jericho (Jordan), there was 'pre-pottery Neolithic'. It is possible, too, that even in the Mesolithic there was some domestication of animals, but that did not add up to a Neolithic Age. In Denmark some food-gathering folk used or made pots; the general view is that they picked up the idea from Neolithic neighbors, but again this does not mean that they were at a Neolithic stage.

The beginner should give much thought to this step in the evolution of man's culture. The study of the Neolithic is the key to much in the study of human society and its environment. The important thing for the beginner to grasp is that the Neolithic did not take place at one time and that it did not begin at any one center. Some peoples, like the Australian Aborigines, never reached the Neolithic stage.

Early Neolithic pottery: top, from Hacilar; middle and bottom, from Siyalk

Man and Animals

Archeologists often find animal bones in prehistoric and historic sites. It is not enough to record types and numbers of bones and stop at that, since an enormous amount of interpretation is required. Are the bones of domestic or wild animals? Is the presence of bones accidental, due to some ritual or evidence of man's diet? Or all three?

It is difficult to determine whether a sheep's remains are of a domesticated animal except by careful analysis of the bones. There are times when it is difficult to distinguish a sheep's bone from a goat's. Very often the only

Above: early sheep. Below: an early domestic dog

clue about domestication comes from prehistoric models in clay.

In some deposits, animal and mollusk remains are an indication of climate. A turtle or a shellfish may indicate a warmer or a colder climate. Bones of an elk, a lemming, a polar bear or a mammoth indicate a cold climate, while monkey, pig, antelope and vole bones help indicate mild conditions. The archeologist who knows little about animals is at a disadvantage. He should at least be able to recognize whether a rabbit or a mole has disturbed a layer.

It is possible that in the Neolithic and later, man learned more than once to domesticate a particular species of animal. The pig and the dog are examples of animals that were domesticated in different places at different times. It is hard to say which animal was the first to join man. Sheep, goats and pigs began to be controlled by man in the Near East before 6000 B.C.—roughly at the same time as full-scale plant cultivation began. Some workers claim that there is strong evidence from Shanidar in northern Iraq that the sheep was domesticated by 9000 B.C.

By 6000 B.C., there were domesticated cattle browsing in Anatolia and elsewhere. Whether these were the first domesticated breeds, only future excavations can tell us. The dog is thought to have been domesticated in the Meso-lithic, but it is difficult to distinguish the bones of these animals from those of foxes and wolves.

Wild ancestors of modern domesticated animals

Early grain types
and flint sickle

Man and Plants

While it is easy to grasp what plant cultivation implies—the saving of seeds and the working of the soil, together with knowledge of seed propagation—the story of how man in the Old and the New World learned to cultivate and select plants for breeding is far from clear.

The archeologist finds evidence of grains that are larger than the wild variety; he also finds sickles and objects that might be taken for hoes. It is possible that sickles might have been used for gathering wild plants. If the grains or fruit are of a plant species that is consistently larger than the wild variety, then we are on the way to recognizing cultivated plant remains. But size is not the main indication. Some of the first Neolithic farmers and horticulturalists may have selected small plants for their power to survive bad weather conditions, for their flavor, for their ability to hold out against the competition of weeds, or even conceivably for some feature such as color that was important for magic. There are many cases where it may be said that plants cultivated man.

When and where were the first plants cultivated or domesticated? From currently available evidence it seems likely that by 9000–8000 B.C.—which is not long after the end of the Pleistocene glaciations of the north —there was cereal agriculture in the Near East, mainly between southeastern Anatolia and the west of Iran. The early wheats, emmer and einkorn, which were found at Jarmo and at Çatal Hüyük, and other food grasses such as barley were quickly established and cultivated.

In Mexico squashes and peppers were on the way to being domesticated between 7000 and 5000 B.C. Corn was being cultivated in Mexico and Central America, perhaps in the 4th millennium B.C., but man was already gathering tiny wild corn, of a type now extinct, inside the period 5000–3500 B.C. This wild corn cob was only a couple of inches long.

Plants domesticated by New World peoples included corn and squash. At right, cultivated corn compared with wild variety.

Man and Pots

The number of people who have lived since Neolithic man began to make pottery in earnest—say from about 6500 B.C.—is prodigious. Multiply that figure by ten (or what figure you wish) to suggest how many pots may have been made for each person, and imagine the astronomical result. *The clay used for many of these pots is still in existence,* since pottery fragments are so durable. Clearly the archeologist must learn all he can from so common an artifact.

How pottery was first invented is difficult to say. Man in the Upper Paleolithic had learned to bake clay objects. Some people have argued that pottery was discovered when a sunbaked vessel was accidentally fired, but evidence for this is not easy to find. It is more likely that in the helpful social and economic climate of the Neolithic, pottery could

Ceramic history: a boundless topic for archeology

Neolithic pottery: upper left from Spain; upper right from Yugoslavia; lower left from China; lower right from Turkey

be invented several times under the sedentary conditions possible at the time. Some early vessels may have been sun-dried. Most scholars are prepared to accept that pottery was independently invented in America some time after 3000 B.C. The change it brought into man's life is indubitable. (Soup and beer became possible for the first time!)

The archeologist has to be aware that some peoples have ceased to make pottery. This has happened in the isles of the Pacific, in medieval Scotland, in pre-colonial Africa and elsewhere. Wood, leather, horn, stone and, later, metal vessels may have been used at certain times since they are less fragile than pottery.

A good archeologist must be familiar with the basic techniques of ceramics. He should, for example, understand the methods by which pottery was made without a wheel — as it always was in ancient America. A potter's wheel of some sort or other was in use in Mesopotamia between 3500 and 3000 B.C. The potter's wheel arrived in Britain just before the Romans came, but in Saxon times pots were again made without the wheel. Techniques seem to come and go and return.

Neolithic pottery details. Top: Hacilar and Thessaly. Center: India. Bottom: Kenya

Neolithic Life

The word Stone Age gives the average person the idea of a 'primitive' world in a state of barbarism. It is important therefore to realize that Neolithic (or New Stone Age) Man was sometimes more than a primitive agriculturist and pastoralist who happened also to have pots. We must also recall that the Neolithic lasted in some areas for over 5,000 years.

First, Neolithic Man was a clever craftsman. He was, for example, a great carpenter and could, even with stone tools, make planks with dowel holes in them. Men and women could weave clothes and stitch them together, and make baskets and mats. Many other techniques were probably at his disposal, though evidence for this is uncertain. For example, the cereals that came into his diet may have made him appreciate salt. Some archeologists have been investigating the possibility that salt was even used as an object of trade.

Perhaps the most unusual aspect of the skills of Neolithic Man was his practicality as a geological prospector. In Britain, for example, he learned to mine through chalk with antler picks to get at high-grade flints. But this is not his only skill. In an island off Northern Ireland there is an isolated spot where there is a small vein of hard blue-gray rock. Some Neolithic prospector learned to ferret this out and to quarry this hard stone for ultimate manufacture as polished axes—one of which was traded as far as the Thames Valley. How the stone was shipped is hard to say, but Neolithic ships must have been seaworthy vessels to enable Britain and Ireland to be 'colonized' in the first place.

Early Neolithic Man built cities and could be adept at walled town defenses. In some lands he produced a lively art, especially clay figurines of deities or animals.

While places like Jericho and Çatal Hüyük are recognized as spectacular Asian examples of urban cultures (Neolithic Man 'invented' cities), it is possible that great Neolithic towns may yet be found in Europe and elsewhere.

In a way, too, it can be said that Neolithic Man discovered the use of metal and thus created the age of metal. Perhaps we may discover one day, too, that writing was first devised in the Neolithic Age of more than one land.

Ax rough-out, Wales. Textile, Hacilar. Flint mine, England.

An early
Neolithic
burial

The Early Neolithic in the Near East

The Proto-Neolithic in the Near East is regarded as beginning about 9000 B.C. What and where was this Proto-Neolithic? There are many examples. We may cite the Natufians of Palestine who hunted gazelles and other animals but had a taste for a cereal diet and used small flints mounted as teeth in bone sickles to reap food plants. Some Natufians (as at Eynan) had villages of about 50 stone-walled houses. They had no pottery but already they made stone pots. At about the same time there were similar Proto-Neolithic cultures 500 miles away at Shanidar in Iraq.

Between 8000 and 7000 B.C., a development of the Natufian culture produced a town of around 10 acres at Jericho. The houses were neatly made of mud bricks and the 'city' walls and towers were of stone. Jericho then had agriculture but no pottery; gazelle-hunting was the main source of protein rather than cattle-keeping. Few would grudge the term 'Neolithic' to Jericho.

After 7000 B.C. a new (pre-pottery) Neolithic culture took

The early Neolithic township of Khirokitia, Cyprus

over Jericho and enlarged it. In Asia Minor and in Iraq there were similar pre-pottery Neolithic cultures about 7000 B.C. Around 6000 B.C., pre-pottery Neolithic folk had sailed successfully to Cyprus and settled there. And by 6500 B.C., pottery was being made in Asia Minor and elsewhere. Pottery then appears in Iran, Syria and at Jarmo in Iraq a little before 6000 B.C.

Perhaps the most astonishing evidence of the progress made by Neolithic man was the development of Çatal (pronounced 'Chatal') Hüyük in southeastern Asia Minor. This town, begun about 6500 B.C., lasted almost 1,000 years, but there were many rebuildings, as can be expected with mud-brick buildings. The houses of this city, which lay near an active volcano, were neatly planned and remarkably standardized. The people of Catal Hüyük were cattle-keepers and agriculturalists who sowed a great variety of wheats. They had elaborate sanctuary buildings with complex rituals and an impressive accompanying art. Perhaps more cities will be discovered in the Middle East and in Europe as well.

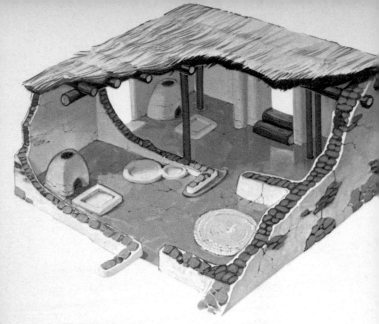

A Neolithic house at Hacilar in Anatolia

The Neolithic in the Near East spreads
Around 5500 B.C., a Neolithic way of life ranged from Iran
to the mainland of Greece. By this time there was such a
variety of cultures that it is impossible to trace influences.
Everywhere there seems to be growth and expansion. We
have evidence of trade and movements, and there must have
been an expansion of peoples looking for further fields and
pastures.

Towns like Hacilar (from before 6000 B.C.), some 200
miles west of Çatal Hüyük, were more ambitious. Occasional
copper objects and marbles and similar games were found,
and most art objects excavated show great sophistication
—while northern Europe was still at food-gathering, Mesolithic stage. Hacilar was deserted by 5000 B.C. Asia Minor
will doubtless furnish other sites of this kind.

Since Mesopotamia, the land between the Euphrates
and the Tigris, was to be the seed-bed of the first civilizations, it is worth sketching, however briefly, some of the
Neolithic cultures of that area. Some cultural features had
spread very widely. For example, pottery of the Halaf type

(about 5000 B.C.) can be found from Syria to Iran. The Halaf culture, which showed glimmerings of the use of copper and all the traits of a prosperous way of life, was displaced by invaders of the 'Ubaid culture before 4300 B.C.

The 'Ubaid culture developed strongly in Mesopotamia and it was at this time that cast bronze axes were made. But most important was the development of social and economic organization, which had as its visible product the gigantic mud-brick temples of Eridu or Tepe Gawra. Organization of religion, agriculture and trade requires records, and by 3500 B.C. there were clay tablets with writing on them. It is not surprising that the words and topics refer to gods, kings, weights, sheep. There were over 30 signs for different kinds of sheep almost at the beginning of writing.

The Uruk period (3500–2900 B.C.) followed, a time when numerous cities came into being. In the Uruk period arose the civilization of Sumeria.

The word 'Neolithic' has been in use just over 100 years; it is becoming clear that in the next ten years we shall learn more about it than we did in the last hundred.

Jericho man reconstructed from a plastered Jericho skull

Neolithic art from Afghanistan and Indus Valley

Neolithic: Africa and Asia

The first Neolithic settlers in Africa appeared in the Nile valley and in parts of Libya, probably between 5000–4500 B.C. The sites that have been discovered—for example in the Fayum, and later ones in the Sudan—show evidence of a variety of cultures with skilled flint industries, good pottery, cattle herding and agriculture. The spread after that was slower because of physical barriers. In parts of Africa below the Equator there was no true Neolithic and only a late, gradual transfer from Middle Stone Age cultures to Late Stone Age cultures with animal herding and some agriculture. This was often the state of affairs until iron came.

But there were some notable diffusions of Neolithic ways to certain parts of Africa. Examples include arrivals in West Africa, notably the Cape Verde area, the Congo and equatorial forest areas (Tumban culture). The forest environments of this kind have not unexpectedly furnished evidence of polished stone axes for forest clearance. Other examples of African Neolithic cultures are the Gumban and Njoroan of East Africa. These well-equipped pastoral cultures of Kenya and neighboring areas used a variety of well-made artifacts such as polished axes, pestles and mortars. Unfortunately, dating is difficult and the time-range can only be put tentatively as 3000–500 B.C. Some of these cultures eventually received or made iron goods without going through a copper or bronze age.

The Neolithic of the Indian subcontinent is thought to have its roots in Afghanistan, Baluchistan, and Sind. Archeologists continually discuss these regions' connections with Iran and Mesopotamia but evidence for links is still tenuous. It is almost certain that in northern Afghanistan a pottery Neolithic culture of some sort was in existence as early as 5300 B.C. By 2600 B.C. or thereabouts, farming and stockbreeding was well established in the Indus valley. It was in this valley that there arose a great civilization with great cities and its own system of writing. One of these cities was more than a mile across. Most readers have heard of Harappa in the Punjab and Mohenjo-daro in Sind, both in Pakistan. This civilization, as impressive

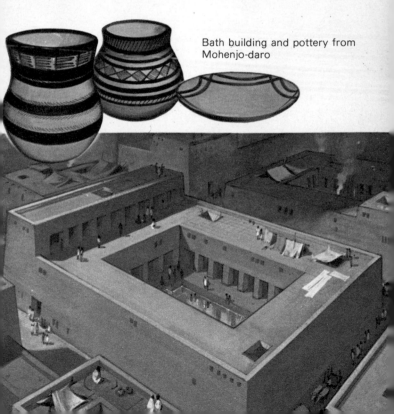

Bath building and pottery from Mohenjo-daro

for its planning and organization as for its plumbing, has not yet been completely dated, but a peak period of about 2300–1750 B.C. has been suggested.

The Neolithic of southern Siberia is in some ways analogous to that of Iran and nearby areas, where cultures like Mesolithic ones developed settled ways of life around 5000 B.C. At sites like Jeitun in Turkmenia, near the Iran border, one may find blades, microliths, bone sickles with flint teeth and a gaily painted pottery. The Siberian Neolithic of the Baikal area dates from about 3000 B.C. onward. It had bone points of seemingly Upper Paleolithic type together with a distinctive pottery, some of it possessing impressions of nets pressed against it. The later Siberian cultures of the Lena area are thought to be ancestral, if only collaterally ancestral, to certain early pottery-using cultures of Canada and the United States, which might have come into existence independently of the Central American pottery makers.

The Neolithic in China may have arisen among Mesolithic peoples in the north of the country as early as 5000 B.C. We are able to distinguish only the main groups. Some of the earliest finds of items made or used by Neolithic folk are from the Ordos desert of Inner Mongolia, and in Manchuria. Possibly better dated is the Yangshao of the Yellow River area which is thought to have begun about 3000 B.C. Yangshao pottery is skillfully made and shows traces of turning. The patterns on these pots are lively. By the time that the Lung-shan culture of about

Neolithic stone implements from China

Kansu Neolithic pots from China

2000 B.C. was established, we find a thin-walled black pottery which shows possible evidence of the use of the wheel. At about this time there may have been emigration into Malaysia and the Pacific.

In Japan the full story of the Neolithic has not yet been worked out, but the Neolithic pottery of the Jomôn period appears to begin very early, perhaps before 4000 B.C.

New World Cultures

America's prehistory is in some respects very different from that of the Old World. It is often easier to refer to it as the 'Pre-Columbian' period, since it is the coming of Columbus that marks the end of America's prehistory.

After 2000 B.C. in South and Middle America we find evidence of villages and what goes under the name of 'ceremonial centers'. The earliest of these centers appear to have been in Peru, but the really striking ones were in

Mexico where, after 1000 B.C., impressive circular, stepped mounds acted as centers for highly organized communities. One of the better-known of these was the Olmec ceremonial site (c. 1000–400 B.C.) to be found at La Venta on an island in Tabasco, Mexico.

At about the same time temple centers, often of ambitious stonework, were established in Peru. Cotton was cultivated there before 1000 B.C., and the later textiles of the South Americans before Columbus were some of the finest weaves ever made by man.

While it is possible to discuss the story of the cultures of Peru and Mexico as distinct units, the ancient peoples of the United States are difficult to isolate or classify. The distinctive pottery of the so-called 'Woodland' cultures has a date range spreading from nearly 1000 B.C.

Three animals that early South Americans made use of: llama, alpaca, and vicuna

Many of our food plants (grown both here and now all over the world) were originally cultivated by early peoples of the Americas. Examples are: corn (maize), tomatoes, potatoes (both regular and sweet), squash.

to A.D. 800. One may note here their huge mounds (either for rituals or for burials) and their elegant stone tobacco pipes. Not all the 'Woodland' peoples were agriculturalists; some were hunters because of the short summer.

Another group of traditions is exemplified by the Mogollon (roughly 100 B.C. to A.D. 1500), the Hohokam (roughly 100 B.C.–A.D. 1400) and the Anazazi (after 100 B.C.–A.D. 1700). These were centered in Arizona, New Mexico and Colorado.

The Mogollon were well organized in their agriculture and in their villages and had well-designed houses. The Anazazi culture has become familiar because of its skills in basket-making and for the complex villages (pueblos) in which they lived. The desert-based Hohokam (who had links with Mexico) produced pots as gay and varied as the best in Old World cultures.

American and European archeology have many useful parallels.

Fall of the Pre-Columbians

In Middle America, the culture that produced the great ceremonial centers such as La Venta and Monte Alban in Oaxaca, Mexico and the gigantic sculptures of the period 1200–600 B.C. has been labeled 'Olmec'. This was one tradition among several of a priestly or theocratic world that persisted until the coming of the Spaniards. In the Yucatan peninsula of Mexico there arose the Maya, a civilization which had its first stages as early as 600 B.C. although the classic period was between about 250 and 900 A.D. It was a culture that depended spiritually not merely on the gods but on the fertility of corn. Their picture writing largely eludes us but their calendar system has been understood enough to show us that in some ways it was more accurate than anything the Romans or Greeks had achieved.

In Mexico there also arose the culture represented by the huge city of Teotihuacan, a great pilgrimage and market center. The Teotihuacan civilization lasted from about 300 B.C. to about 600 A.D., when the city was destroyed.

As elsewhere, these civilizations were eclipsed or destroyed by 'barbarians'. Warriors largely displaced priestly rulers. Thus it was that the Toltecs and the Mixtecs ruled in Mexico until they allowed a small tribe a toehold in the Valley of Mexico. This group, a group of perhaps only a thousand originally, was known as the Aztecs. Gathering strength in the 12th century A.D., these peoples (who shared both the organizational skills and the hunger for power of the Romans and the Normans) established a great empire that was defeated in the 16th century, ironically, by a small group of Spaniards.

In South America, a minor kingdom of the Andes that flourished just before 1000 A.D. began to consolidate and a smaller group, the Incas, which had begun to expand around 1200 A.D., staged an aggressive expansion in the 15th century. They had just settled their dynastic squabbles when Francesco Pizarro in 1532–33 conquered the whole empire with a handful of men.

Items made in the 2,000-year period in the Americas before Columbus

Neolithic pots from the Danube basin

Neolithic Cultures Enter Europe

Well before 5000 B.C. the first farmers had established themselves in northern Greece. In the next thousand years the Neolithic way of life spread as far as the Low Countries. It took another thousand years in order to complete the spread of the New Stone Age to the British Isles, Scandinavia and western Europe.

The first arrivals brought with them much that reminds us of their Near Eastern origins: some used mud bricks and others had inscribed objects of eastern origins. But as these farmers and shepherds spread up the river valley of southeastern Europe, and especially the Danube area, they developed pottery and other features that were genuinely European. Some groups were probably more mobile than others and may have moved on because they had exhausted the soil, but others stayed put. The site of Karanovo in Bulgaria was occupied for over 3,000 years and the 'tell', or heap of successive deposits, is over 40 feet high.

In the fifth millennium B.C. Central Europe witnessed an important group called the 'Linear' pottery culture because of the distinctive pottery. However, they also deserve our attention for the long rectangular houses (some over 100 feet long) clustered into 'villages'. Meanwhile, Neolithic cultures had been established in southern Italy and eastern Spain.

The main pattern, however, which finally crystallized in Europe between 4000 and 2500 B.C., resolved itself into (1) a 'Western' group, including among others the Chassey-Cortaillod cultures of France and Switzerland, the wares of the western Mediterranean, which were decorated with shell-edge impressions (impressed ware), and the British Early Neolithic cultures; (2) the Danish and northern German areas with the strange 'Funnel Beakers' and (3) the Boian (Romania) and Tripolye (Ukraine) cultures.

Trade of some sort was promoted throughout Neolithic Europe, at first in shells and stone and possibly salt; later on, but before 2500 B.C., copper from the Carpathians and elsewhere was being traded and used.

A typical house of Neolithic Europe (reconstructed from clay models) and Neolithic European artifacts—ax, bone comb, and tomb figures

The Neolithic in Northern Europe

In Poland and Germany the first Neolithic arrivals were well established between 5000 and 4000 B.C. Their origins can be found in the earlier Danubian Neolithic. In the Schleswig-Holstein area, which lies between Denmark and Germany, the Ellerbek culture (4500–4000 B.C.) has ample marks of a Neolithic way of life: wood spades, pots with conical bottoms, ceramic oil lamps, etc. Knowledge of pot-making seeped through to the Mesolithic Ertebølle people in Denmark, who were generally food-gatherers, depositing vast middens of shell remains.

In the Rhineland we find around 4000 B.C. a culture, named after a place called Rossen, with a distinctive pottery and houses of an unusual trapezoid-shaped plan. A little to the north of this area there then developed cultures that had common features, found in a band running from Holland to Poland. Among these features is the so-called Funnel Beaker of around 3500 B.C. Saxony in Germany has produced many remains of this culture. These cultures are not the direct ancestors of the British Neolithic. A further mingling of cultures took place before the mix was ready for emigrations to Britain.

Switzerland and northern France both received a full Neolithic before 3500 B.C.; in northern France there was a transition from pick-using cultures, such as the Campignian, which merged into such groups as the Chassey culture. Many early Neolithic cultures in France contain geometric microliths harking back to the Mesolithic.

Of great importance in the development of a northern Neolithic is the development in northern Germany, the Netherlands and southern Sweden, of 'passage graves'. These huge stone burial structures (generally built after 3000 B.C.) are also found in France, Britain, Spain and part of the north coasts of the western Mediterranean. But there are distinctive local features in the northern zone, although the basic type is still a circular or many-angled burial chamber with an approach passage serving some ritual or social requirement.

After this, the Neolithic in the North becomes more and more complex, and varied pots and burial customs pose enormous problems for prehistorians.

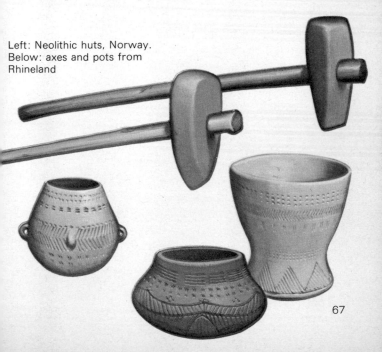

Left: Neolithic huts, Norway.
Below: axes and pots from Rhineland

The Neolithic in Some Mediterranean Lands

Like most human occurrences, the entry of the first farmers and shepherds into southern Europe was an untidy process. Although some of the earliest arrivals were in the Danube area and Greece, we find no simple fanning out from bridgeheads. Irregular, sporadic arrivals at separate spots seem to have been the method employed, although this may be only the picture coming from the accidents of discovery. In Italy, for example, the new settlers seem to have chosen Liguria and parts of Italy's deep south not long after 5000 B.C., and Sicily and Malta were not far behind in receiving independent settlers. We have to gain more knowledge, though, before we can say what sorts of boats were used and how they selected new areas in which they were going to settle.

France, after the artistic glories of its Upper Paleolithic, may have become a backwater of Mesolithic cultures for a long time. The first clearly defined makers of pots were on the scene around 4500–4000 B.C.

The details of the arrival of the Neolithic in Greece are still being sorted out and there have been many unexpected features. In Thessaly, remains of the equipment and daily doings of a *pre-pottery* Neolithic have been found and attested; this culture goes back to before 6000 B.C. Enough features have been found to enable us to see ultimate links with the way of life in Cyprus or ancient Jericho. At that time prospectors for obsidian (a mineral used for tools) were ranging through some of the Greek isles.

In many ways, Spain and Portugal offer the most challenges to students of the Neolithic. There had been varied, strong Mesolithic cultures in this peninsula from the beginning of the post-glacial period. The mingling that occurred with Neolithic newcomers just before 4000 B.C. enabled the original inhabitants to maintain some of their old ways. For example, the rock paintings that are descendants of the ancient art of the Paleolithic now appear to show animals led by cords. Perhaps it was in these times in Spain, Malta and elsewhere, that those who organized the burying of their dead began to evolve attitudes and techniques that later came to fruition in the form of burials beneath stones.

Neolithic objects from Spain
with conjectural reconstruction
of mixed farming and hunting
activities

This is a reconstruction of a British Neolithic causewayed camp although based on archeological evidence, it may be misleading.

The First Farmers in Britain

Some time before 3500 B.C., the first Neolithic settlers came to the British Isles. Where they came from is difficult to say, but evidence from related pottery found abroad has been thought to show links with France, the Low Countries and even Germany. Among the earlier settlements (around 3500 B.C. dated by radiocarbon) are Windmill Hill in Wiltshire and Hembury in Devon, in England, and in Ireland, at Dalkey Island, County Dublin.

One school of thought has argued very plausibly that Mesolithic British food-gatherers gradually learned the Neolithic way of life from the newcomers and gradually became Neolithic (or 'Secondary Neolithic'). However, the highly pitted decorations of the Secondary Neolithic pots are very different from the generally plain Windmill Hill pots. Others have argued that the Early British Neolithic (such as at Windmill Hill), and the 'Secondary' wares found in the Thames and in the East Midlands were parallel developments of broadly the same cultures as the Windmill Hill 'Western' group.

One of the better known features of the early Neolithic of Britain are the 'causewayed camps', which are concentric enclosures, some of them hundreds of feet in diameter. The rings of ditches are broken by 'causeways'. Some have suggested that they are ritual sites, and others that they are tribal centers, periodic meeting places for exchange of goods and for ceremonies. Among the better-known examples of causewayed camps are Windmill Hill and Hembury. These structures are similar to causewayed camps in the early French Neolithic.

The first Neolithic settlers had varied funerary practices. Some burials, perhaps of chiefs, were twofold. First the corpse might have a spell in a mortuary enclosure; then it would go into a long barrow of earth. At about the same time, burials were introduced that used great stone slabs (megaliths) for structures known as 'chamber tombs'.

Neolithic items from Britain

monument, the remains of which still exist today. The site was then a circular area surrounded by a ditch and an inner bank made from its spoil. There was a ring of 56 'ritual' holes ringing the inside. The next stage of Stonehenge was in the Beaker period.

Avebury, also in southwestern England, has been called a 'henge', although this huge structure — over 450 yards across — has many unusual features, including a great ditch and an avenue marked by stone uprights. A ritual center of this kind must have had a complex history and the whole monument was probably not built at one time. Most of the evidence points to the place being constructed mainly around 2000 B.C. or a century or two later.

The end of the Neolithic in Britain is, theoretically, marked by the first arrival of copper with the Beaker people.

Avebury, another Neolithic ritual site in England

Later Neolithic Britain

Almost entirely a British phenomenon, although there are some continental parallels, are the ritual sites called henges. Basically they are circular ditches with one or more entrances; the sizes vary. Many of them show evidence of an internal ring of pits, which were sometimes the sockets for uprights of timber or stone. They range across the later Neolithic of England and Scotland, a period roughly between 2100 and 1600 B.C. Some famous henges are of the Beaker period at the end of the Neolithic. In northern Britain there are many stone circles which are still little understood, and even more mysterious are the so-called processional ways, or *cursuses,* such as are found in Wiltshire and in Continental Europe.

The famous 'temple' of Stonehenge was started at the end of the Neolithic, about 1800 B.C. It was not the impressive

The earliest Stonehenge—about 1800 B.C.

Megaliths

Archeologists have found megalithic (from the Greek words *megas*, great and *litho*, stone) chambered tombs to be an important source of information. In western Europe they are found from Spain to Scandinavia, from the Orkneys to Sardinia and Apulia, dating from the early Neolithic to the end of the Bronze Age. Megaliths and stone cists have also been used in India's Iron Age, on Easter Island, in nineteenth-century Africa and in many other places. This is not evidence of interconnected cultures or movements but simply of availability of stone and man's almost universal desire at one time or another to build worthy houses for his dead. In any case there is so much variety in megaliths — from the cist tombs of Bronze Age Japan to the Hunebedden of the Netherlands and from Maes Howe in Britain to the Cueva de Menga in Spain — that it is impossible to generalize about their general structure, dating or function. Some megalithic tombs were used for a thousand years.

Other tombs have been looted or altered and many megaliths have been re-used over the years.

One British group is the 'gallery graves' from the west of Britain. This is a *gallery* or chamber of stone slabs, sometimes with side compartments; a mound of earth or stones covered the whole. The West Kennet long barrow in Wiltshire is a typical example. The other group is the 'passage grave' of which Maes Howe, Orkney, is a fine example.

The archeologist excavating chamber tombs has to be vigilant in looking for evidence of rituals (fires, food, broken items) at the entrance; he also has to distinguish the successive heapings of bones or bodies taken from mortuary houses.

A major Neolithic megalithic grave in Ireland—New Grange. Left: viewed from the air. Below: a carving at the entrance and, right, the interior.

Prehistoric Burials

Man's way of burying his dead in the Neolithic varied from land to land. Already in the Mesolithic, funerary practices varied from burials in containers to the specialized collective burials of skulls. Burials ranged from casual dumping to interments of great complexity. In Britain a skeleton scattered through the ditch of a Neolithic causewayed camp might indicate indifference or violence. In Neolithic Japan a flexed body is buried in a shell midden. A touch of ceremony or sentiment is added by placing at the head a jar containing an infant's bones.

Sometimes a burial is 'secondary': the body has been re-buried some time after death and after considerable decay has gone on. This has been noted in many Neolithic cultures from Britain (in megaliths) and America to the earlier Jericho.

Cremations have often been thought to have been introduced in the Bronze Age, but there are many Neolithic examples, such as in Greece where bodies were partially burned before burial not long after 5000 B.C. In Poland cremations of just after 4000 B.C. were noted, and in the late Neolithic of

Neolithic flexed burial, China

Remains of a cremation from the Iron Age in Finland

Czechoslovakia cremations were side by side with unburnt burials. In Germany cremations were found under Neolithic houses. Cremation was practiced throughout the American continent over 2000 years ago, and there are isolated examples of a late Stone Age site in Kenya (about 1000 B.C.) where elaborate cremation rites went on.

Throughout his researches, the archeologist must try to understand the mixed motives behind burials: placation of the dead, getting the help of the dead, helping the dead on their journey and equipping them for the afterlife. He must learn to distinguish between continuing traditions and the custom of later peoples putting their dead in a megalith or barrow constructed a thousand years before.

A burial must not be studied merely for its jewelry, pottery and ritual paraphernalia. Burials—in particular, family groups and cemeteries—can teach the researcher much about disease, growth, nutrition and heredity.

THE AGE OF METALS BEGINS

Archeologists in the past made too sharp a distinction between the Stone Age and the Bronze Age. In fact, copper was probably the first metal man used, and even copper was not instantly adopted. Most cultures went through a stage when stone tools were used side by side with those of copper. The term Chalcolithic Age ('copper-stone') has been used to denote this stage. At Hacilar and Catal Hüyük in Asia Minor there was some copper in use, mainly for ornaments, around 5500 B.C. and in some cases a thousand years earlier. Perhaps this was hardly a true chalcolithic period, but at Siyalk in Iran, and at Uruk in Iraq, copper implements were in use at the same time as stone a little before 3500 B.C. In Britain, at the end of the third millennium B.C. the Beaker Folk had metal daggers, but they also put traditional flint daggers and arrowheads into their burials. In the Deccan, India, in the middle of the second millennium B.C. people used blade tools of flintlike chert but they also had elegant fish hooks of copper and cast shaft-axes.

The copper ore malachite (upper right) was smelted and then poured into a stone mold to make an axhead.

Copper ores are sometimes blue or green, so once the art of smelting copper was discovered it was easy for prospectors to seek out more ores. Iron or tin have less obvious ores.

While copper is not a hard metal, it is possible to make more efficient tool edges with it than with stone. Man swiftly learned to use the metal efficiently and economically. A central midrib in a slim dagger increased strength but cut out unnecessary use of expensive metal. Arrowheads could quickly be given sharp barbs, and tools such as saws become more practical when metal became available.

In America, man learned to use copper in a different way. For example, in Wisconsin the 'Old Copper' Indians made knives, awls, barbed harpoons and fishhooks of copper not long after 3000 B.C. But they did not smelt the copper. Instead they mined 'native copper' which was found, without needing smelting, in volcanic and other rocks. This copper was hammered or, perhaps, heated and hammered. The Incas, too, worked in copper and indeed in gold, silver, tin and lead.

Copper tools of the 'Old Copper' culture in Wisconsin, c. 3000 B.C.

The Bronze Age

Even when bronze—an alloy of copper and tin—came into use, stone arrowheads and scrapers still went on being used. But there is no doubt that the introduction of this alloy was accompanied by, and indeed helped to bring about, a number of crucial changes so that the term 'Bronze Age', like Neolithic Age, serves to denote a basic stage in human cultures.

The period 3000–2000 B.C. was the time when bronze came to be widely used in the Old World. In America, some copper and bronze working was devised before the appearance of the Europeans. In Colombia, in South America, a gold and copper alloy was worked. Bronze reached the extremes of the Old World roughly at about the same time—in Britain, around 1800 B.C. and China, around 1500 B.C. The Chinese had already used copper for almost a thousand years.

Bronze was never cheap, since the copper and the tin of the alloy usually had to come from different places. Scrap bronze was therefore a valuable commodity and we still hear about new finds of 'hoards' left by itinerant bronzesmiths. Such hoards contain an extraordinary variety of objects, ranging from trumpet mouthpieces to cattle bells. They offer a useful cross-dating for objects.

It is ironical to find that in Europe, Asia and Africa some of the finest bronze work—such as hammered plate shields or cauldrons—is of the Iron Age. This is often what happens: when a material is eclipsed, its technologists reach high peaks of craftsmanship and technique. Bronze often survives in the soil much better than iron, so it might be possible for us to obtain a rather misleading picture about the extent to which it was used.

Bronze was generally cast in molds of clay, stone or other materials. Elaborate casting was done by making a wax or wood model and embedding it in clay. Metal poured into the mold with the wax model melted out the wax and left the shape in the clay mold. Bronze in the Bronze Age of the Old World was sometimes cold-worked by hammering. Lead was used as an additive in both Europe and Egypt, possibly to help flow into the mold.

Bronze hoard from Leicestershire, England, of about the 7th century B.C.

Ingots from a Bronze Age shipwreck.

Early Metal Cultures: Asia and Europe

Southern Turkestan is not an area well known to many Western archeologists, but a considerable knowledge of a complex Neolithic way of life is emanating from the U.S.S.R. Some of these Neolithic cultures (roughly between 5300 and 4300 B.C.) already used axes of copper and spearheads of the same metal. This was the 'Namazga II' culture, and there were similar ones in Asia working toward a complete mastery of metal. Metal does not automatically change one culture to another, but in metal we see the potentiality not so much of technical progress as of power struggles and warfare.

In Iran, at Tepe Sialk, before 4500 B.C. hammered native copper items were used; a little later these were annealed. By 4000 B.C. cast metal axes were found there. Bronze went on being used in Asia and elsewhere, even when iron was established in other places. Examples are the elegant bronzes of Luristan, in Iran (after 900 B.C.). The varied weapons and implements of bronze used by the Scythians in southern

Russia around the 7th century B.C. have shapes like those already being made in iron in Europe.

Copper and bronze may have entered Europe as 'personal imports' or as trade from centers in Europe controlled or initiated by traders or prospectors from the eastern Mediterranean. But a proper bronze age needs craftsmen and smiths. What persuaded them to move into Europe? Perhaps their home bases in the Near East were being shaken at that time (just before 2000 B.C.) by internal unrest or barbarian attacks. Whatever the reason, smiths, craftsmen and eventually bronze scrap-merchants were soon established in Europe.

There is no doubt that trade became an important element of Bronze Age life, but details often must be inferred. Only rarely have shipwrecks been found like that off Cape Gelidonya, in Turkey. This little ship, sunk around 1200 B.C., not only had a varied load of ingots and other goods, but also a set of 'international' weights for handling business in many countries. By then trade extended from the Baltic areas and Britain through much of Europe to the Mediterranean.

Remains of Bronze Age Europe include amber and gold beads, from various parts, and Scandinavian boat types drawn on rocks.

Three Bronze Age cultures are represented by a Hittite gate, a Mycenaean dagger and a Minoan idol.

Bronze Age Cultures and Civilizations of the Mediterranean

By 2000 B.C., several of the great civilizations were well established. Egypt was entering its twelfth dynasty and Babylon had begun its first great dynasty, which was to reach its zenith in the reign of Hammurabi (1792–1750 B.C.). In Crete the 'Middle Minoan' period produced buildings so bold in their concept and organization that the word 'palace' has to be used in describing the residences of this civilization, which was based on large-scale, efficient trading. The dating and culture of the Minoans are being reconsidered.

The Bronze Age of Greece, generally known as the Helladic period, was pre-Greek, but already the national skill in pottery and sculpture was foreshadowed. It is assumed that men began to speak Greek around 1900 B.C. Archeologists are still trying to determine how far the Minoan civilization of Crete was related to the Helladic of Greece. By 1500 B.C., the Mycenaean civilization was rising, with its palaces or fortresses at Mycenae, Tiryns, Pylos and other sites. Cretan power seems to have diminished by 1400 B.C., and the Mycenaeans then lorded it over the Mediterranean as rulers and as traders. As early as 1450 B.C., a system of writing was in use, a script deciphered as being Greek only as recently as in the 1950s. The Mycenaean world is partly depicted in the Homeric poems, although they were put into the form we know in the Iron Age. Troy also existed; indeed there were several Troys, and it is possibly around 1350–1250 B.C. that the Homeric one fell.

About 1200 B.C., there were great disturbances in the east and west of the ancient world. Great empires such as that of the Hittites of Asia Minor collapsed at that time. Mycenaean power lasted a little longer, but by 1050 or 1000 B.C. Mycenaean glory was preserved only in epic poetry and in ruins. Greece and, later, western Asia Minor nevertheless experienced a continuation and development of the culture of the Mycenaeans. The great expansion of the Greeks, whose colonies stretched from the Black Sea to Spain, was in the 8th, 7th and 6th centuries B.C. The great 'classical' period was the 5th century B.C.

Reconstruction of Mycenaean equipment and jewelry

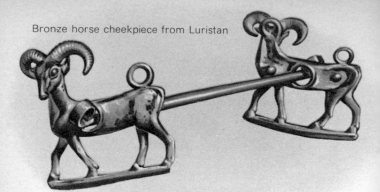

Bronze horse cheekpiece from Luristan

Barbarian Bronze in Europe and Asia

It will take some time before all early metal finds are re-examined to see if they are of copper or bronze. But it is probable that in Mesopotamia bronze was being used occasionally around 3000 B.C. In Iran or the Caspian area, bronze was used early in the third millennium. We should note here that these first users of metal were chalcolithic—that is, they used both metal and stone implements. In India, chalcolithic cultures appeared as early as 2500 B.C., but true bronze was much later. China was using copper at about the same time, but the first significant bronzes are of the Shang dynasty (post 1500 B.C.).

Metal, both copper and bronze was in use in Greece as early as 2400 B.C. It is said that *Cyprus* means 'copper', indicative of the island's rich copper supplies.

Perhaps the chief feature of the Bronze Age in Europe is the quantity of trade by land and sea. A 'Mycenaean' type dagger from Greece has been found in Britain; on Stonehenge itself are carvings of daggers said to have an Aegean ancestry. The wealthy Wessex culture of England has items that also appear in the Únétice culture of Czechoslovakia. Amber from the shores of the Baltic has been found in Greece and Wessex with similar gold decorations.

The horse is thought to have been domesticated in the steppes before 2000 B.C. Very often the domestication of the horse can only be inferred from metal finds such as parts of bridles, cheekpieces, bits, etc. Some antler cheekpieces have been noted in Britain. The date range of such items is around 2000–1500 B.C. Other species like the onager (a sort of donkey) and the ox may have been used quite early to pull carts. There are four-wheeled vehicles illustrated in pictographs drawn in Mesopotamia before 3000 B.C. In Holland, before 2000 B.C., four-wheel wagons trundled over log roads. There is ample evidence, even from the Neolithic, of vehicles shown in models or drawings. Little, however, is known about the origin of the wheel. It seems to have been the result of a deliberate design, not a gradual development.

Two indications of the
Bronze Age: horse-breaking
in Scythia and
pottery from Lausitz
in eastern Europe.

Between 2500 and 2300 B.C., there moved westward from areas behind the Volga various people loosely described by archeologists as being of the *Kurgan* cultures. By 2000 B.C., traces of their influence could be found from Scandinavia to Italy and from eastern France to Asia Minor. Already they had learned of the techniques developed in the Near East for working bronze. They buried their dead in barrows (kurgans) and had not only distinctive axes of stone or metal but also sturdy wagons. The kurgan peoples, along with others, have been claimed as the first bearers of Indo-European speech into Europe.

The cultures that developed from or followed the kurgan makers were numerous. We can mention here only a few of the cultures that should be familiar to serious students of European prehistory. For example, we should be aware of the

Artifacts
from Bronze Age
Europe include:
bronze wheel from
Switzerland; bronze
bit from Germany;
urn from England.

Lighter areas indicate the range of the Urnfield Culture of Europe.

Únétice (or 'Aunjetitz') culture of around 1800–1450 B.C. with its savage weapon, the bronze halberd. This localized culture of Central Europe marks the first time bronze was used on a large scale.

A European example from the Middle Bronze Age is the so-called 'Tumulus cultures'. They developed existing techniques of burying the dead in pits under mounds. Flourishing in areas west of the Únétice area, they reached their peak around 1500–1300 B.C.

Of great archeological interest is the group known by the omnibus title of the 'Urnfield cultures', with a lengthy time-range of 1400–700 B.C. Beginning in the Danube area, and subsequently spreading to central Europe and Italy, this culture (or rather group of cultures) often buried their cremated dead in pits or urn graves, which accumulated into large cemeteries. The cemetery of Lausitz in Silesia has lent its name (as 'Lausitz' or 'Lusatian') to aspects of this culture.

Beakers from Britain and Europe with copper and flint daggers

Beaker Cultures of Europe

At the end of the Neolithic periods (between 2500 and 1800 B.C.), when copper was coming into use in Europe, there appeared peoples who buried their dead with tallish, decorated vessels called 'Beakers' by archeologists. From Britain and Spain to Czechoslovakia and Hungary and as far south as Sicily these vessels were used and imitated. It has been noted that people as vigorous as the Romans and the Normans failed to establish themselves all over the British Isles, yet the Beaker People did manage to do so. The vessels, at least, spread far and wide; it is possible that we have here nothing more unusual than the distribution of the Coca-Cola bottle. We may thus be mistaken in speaking of the Beaker People; it is possible that we have just the traveling of a culture trait.

There is still considerable discussion as to the origin of the Beaker. Some have thought that the vessel type began its career in Spain and Portugal and spread eastward. It has also been argued that there were 'refluxes', which may have brought the Beaker back to the place of its birth.

Although most scholars would say that the Beakers of Britain came from the Low Countries, there are suggestions that France and Spain may have also dispatched either the vessels and their users or the techniques of making and using them. Beaker varieties in Britain vary both in date and in area of distribution.

Along with Beakers we find fine gold ornaments, skillfully made flint daggers and arrowheads as well as copper daggers. While in Mesopotamia and Egypt there were fully developed civilizations, Europe (apart from the Minoan world) was hardly at an advanced stage of culture. Yet in many ways the Beaker People came in as a sort of 'yeast': things started to happen not long after their arrival. They produced a taste for complexity and expansion. The henges of Britain and much of the Stonehenge we know were built in Beaker times. It has even been suggested by serious scholars that Indo-European languages came in to Europe with the Beaker users.

The second phase of Stonehenge, c. 1600 B.C.

Bronze Age Britain

Metalwork found in Britain that can be dated to before 2000 B.C., whether copper or bronze, can be said to have been an import. After that date, and especially after 1800 B.C., some metal objects began to be manufactured in the British Isles.

The plain, flat axes, the broad daggers, the long rapiers and dirks as well as the 'palstave' (a cast ax designed for a split, crook-head wood handle) and many dress accessories form obvious components of the first half of the British Bronze Age. It should not be forgotten that flint arrowheads and certain stone axe-hammers still went on being used while metal was expensive. But within a few centuries, Britain and Ireland began to gain importance for producing bronze and gold objects. A complex typology of bronzework is today keeping many archeologists busy, as is the problem of assessing trade and craft relations between Britain and continental Europe.

The second half of the Bronze Age (in Britain it bumps into the Iron Age around 500 B.C.) produced socketed

Bronze Age pottery-making and spearheads

axes, leaf-shaped slashing swords and a great variety of spearheads. But weapons are not the only finds; there are trumpets, hammers, razors, chisels and, indeed, many unidentified objects still to be found around Britain.

Variations in pottery are too numerous to be listed here, but one can mention a few examples of types. In parts of southern Britain around 1400–900 B.C. appeared a distinctive series of so-called bucket or barrel urns, occasionally going with smaller 'globular' urns. Better known is the 'food vessel' of the period around 1700–1300 B.C., which is found patchily but frequently in all parts of Britain and Ireland. Collared urns (the top is really like a turned-down collar) also are found in many parts of Britain, including Wessex with its wealthy culture of the period 1650–1400 B.C. In northern Britain many urns of the Bronze Age are decorated swags of 'encrusted' ornaments for which Irish parallels have been found. Although it has been difficult to correlate pots and metalwork in Britain, it is easy to visualize great variations in activities and peoples.

Pots and tools of the British Bronze Age

Burial Mounds

'Barrows', 'tumuli' and *'Hügelgraber'* are mounds, generally round, which were built over burials. They were especially common in the Bronze Age, although there were also round barrows in Europe and elsewhere in the Neolithic and in historic periods. 'Long barrows', too, are found in many parts of the world. Mounds of this kind went on being heaped for a long time: the Iron Age Hallstatt warriors of Central Europe also lay under barrows, as did Scythian leaders; American Indian chiefs more than a thousand years before Columbus had mounds of various shapes placed over them. Barrows may also be found in Poland, Albania, Scotland and Japan.

It is impossible to make a general statement that explains why the influential men and women of the past felt their dignity and afterlife would be enhanced by a barrow. So esteemed were barrows that in Britain Romans, Saxons and others inserted their dead into Bronze Age barrows

Schematized 'bell' and 'disc' barrows, two basic burial mounds

Top: an early American Indian mound; bottom: barrows in U.S.S.R.

producing many a problem for the excavator.

So fascinating are barrows that although there are thousands that have survived plowing or erosion, few have not been mauled by plunderers or inept archeologists.

The archeologist who wishes to learn more about barrows soon discovers that they are not simple domes of earth heaped over a burial. Some have ditches around them while others are found to show evidence of a ring of stakes that once encircled it. This is not unexpected, but some barrows skillfully dissected by the archeologist show a complex sequence of events. The corpse might be cremated and a little wooden house put over it for a time; then a stake circle was put round the area; and after an interval soil was heaped over the collapsed hut. After several more stages (which may have included additional burials), the barrow as we see it today was heaped up.

Ritual Sites Before and After the Bronze Age

Many jokes are made about archeologists who are said to explain anything they can't understand or recognize as a 'ritual' object or site. Interpreting even a minor find can be filled with problems. For example, a small hole in the ground containing burnt twigs may have been for a nearby burial—or it may have been a small fire for smoke-curing hides. Signs of ritual behavior, when excavated, are sometimes hard to interpret as such. However, certain features, such as sacrificial burials under structures and similar finds, can occasionally help the archeologist make intelligent suggestions.

Many sites such as the henges of Britain are generally conceded to be of a ritual nature. These circular enclosures, often with timber uprights and occasionally with stone ones, range in time from the Neolithic to the Bronze Age. Often such places were used for centuries. Stonehenge in England began as a timber structure and finally ended

The final stage of Stonehenge, c. 1400 B.C.

up as the impressive structure that has partially survived to this day. Although Stonehenge is one of the more impressive European prehistoric sites, circular structures with superficially similar features have been found in other parts of Europe. A late Iron Age one, for example, has been found in Romania.

The most astonishing claims have been made for both Stonehenge and this Romanian circle. They have been called 'computers' and so on. While it has been shown that some of these structures *may* have had astronomical connections, the reader is urged not to accept the mathematical aspects of these structures without demanding a full explanation—especially when the conclusions are derived with the spurious accuracy that comes from reading angles from a drawing on a reduced scale. Fortunately, many more scientifically trained workers are appearing on the scene, and in the next decade we shall have a truer picture of the mathematical side of megalithic and other structures.

End of the Bronze Age: Europe and Asia

Terms like Bronze Age and Iron Age, it must be repeated, do not carry automatic dating. It depends on what part of the world is being considered. Indeed, the 'Three Ages' system is more often than not an oversimplification.

In China, for example, the first bronze objects emerged sometime around 1500 B.C., as a result of contacts with central Asia. In Britain, bronze had arrived some centuries earlier, in a world probably having a less centralized social organization; but by 1500 B.C. the Shang Dynasty was ruling China, and there are elaborate sites of politico-religious importance such as was found near Anyang in Honan, northern China. The dating of much of this portion of China's story depends on records that are not highly trustworthy until after 1000 B.C. Chinese craftsmanship in working bronze lay not so much in the skilled making of weaponry as in the making of elaborate 'ritual' vessels. Such vessels went on being made for over a thousand years, well after the time the Chinese had learned to make cast iron (about 600–400 B.C.). The rest of the world went on using wrought iron until recent times. Often an invention is made before the economic and cultural climate is ready for it.

Moving back to the West to Greece, for example, we should try to consider what the Late Bronze Age meant in that area. Oddly enough, some of the people who shattered the Bronze Age *status quo* around 1300–1000 B.C. in areas in and around what we now call Greece, were Greeks themselves. It is very hard to sort out which people and what circumstances brought down the Minoan and Mycenaean cultures. The Greeks themselves knew that they were descendants of different groups of incoming Greeks (e.g., the Dorians, Ionians, etc.) who came at different times. So even if the Mycenaean civilization was Greek, as the Linear B tablets indicate, there is no reason why the Bronze Age world of Mycenae should not have been shattered, in that time of troubles, by new Greek invaders.

Typical of the variety of bronze objects are these:
bronze cauldron, China; ax, Luristan; Hallstatt burial urn, Poland;
bronze knifehandle, China

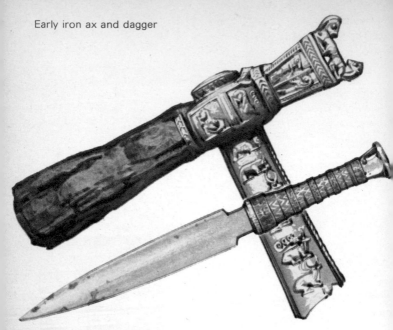

THE IRON AGE

In any generalized account, the Iron Age is supposed to follow the Bronze Age as the latter is supposed to follow the Stone Age. But the beginnings of the Iron Age in various parts of the world are tricky to date, partly because iron corrodes in soil much more than flint or bronze.

The coming of iron to each region of the world was astonishingly varied. In the Pacific, a taste for iron was acquired by the scrounging of nails and other items from European expedition ships such as those of the eighteenth-century Captain James Cook. A European example from 500 B.C. or a little later might be a socketed iron ax found in the Thames river, which is a hammered, wrought version of late Bronze Age socketed axes of Europe.

No pattern of introduction is typical. In China, perhaps at the same time as the Thames ax was made, iron appeared in a cast form and as a mold for bronze tools. As a further lesson in how human cultures vary, we can recall that cast iron did not figure very much in European technology until the second half of the eighteenth century A.D.

Iron was used by Eskimos and by many other peoples in the form of worked meteoritic iron, which often contained an admixture of nickel that made it preferable for tools. The smelting of iron ores was a later development. That copper ores were discovered before iron ores is not surprising, since copper ores can be smelted by heat; iron ores need a good air blast and at first produce rough blooms that have to be hammered and reheated more than once. Hence the term 'wrought' iron.

In the past, prehistorians have with some reason assigned the period 1300–1200 B.C. as the main beginning of iron-working and the Iron Age proper in the Old World. But there is evidence that man was occasionally working iron a thousand years earlier in Anatolia and Mesopotamia

Left: meteoritic iron. Right: iron tool edges from China

and elsewhere. Properly wrought iron was being skillfully produced in the mountains of Armenia by the beginning of the second millennium B.C. Around 1500 B.C., in the lands ruled by the Hittites of Asia Minor, an iron was being made which could be said to have steel-like qualities. The technique of selecting and working ores spread quickly, so that between the years 1200 and 1000 B.C. iron-working extended itself over the Near East as far as Iran, as well as to Greece and Italy.

The ancient Egyptians used iron sporadically but they did not become an 'Iron Age culture' until about 700 B.C. They may well have learned iron-working long after the Phoenicians of Tyre, Sidon and Carthage. Iron spread into Africa very slowly. It was thought that North Africa did not enter the Iron Age until the third or fourth century B.C., while the southern part of Africa did not achieve the general working of iron until the period A.D. 100–600. Recent work on radiocarbon dating in Africa, however, has led to hypotheses that iron may have been used or worked in Africa as early as 900 B.C. African archeology will sup-

An iron hoe and dagger from Africa

Cast iron mold and ax from China

ply many surprises for prehistorians.

In Europe the main impulse for iron-working followed the growth after 700–600 B.C. of the area around Hallstatt in Austria where suitable ores were available. Most of the Iron Age cultures of Europe owe something to Hallstatt.

Iron is thought to have come into general use in India at about the same time as in northern Europe—that is, after 500 B.C.—and in China a little later. However, there is always the probability of new discoveries which will show that there were sporadic introductions before that date. It has been noted that iron was in use in one place in India about 1000 B.C. This is still uncertain, but there is no doubt that India's skill in iron-working developed steadily. The Romans imported ingots of high-grade iron from India. Iron-working always maintained a regional air and technological advances were never widespread, even in the Middle Ages. The next moves forward in the technology of iron did not take place until the eighteenth and nineteenth centuries.

Early Iron-Using Cultures of Europe

The introduction of iron to Europe was not sudden. What really happened was that Bronze Age cultures of Europe gradually began to obtain iron implements or weapons. After the collapse of the Hittite empire in Asia Minor early in the 12th century B.C., the use of iron spread south into Palestine and westward into Greece and the rest of southeastern Europe.

By the end of the 9th century B.C., the so-called Urnfield cultures were reaching their maximum expansion in Central Europe. For convenience, archeologists use the omnibus term 'Hallstatt Culture' to describe the way of life and equipment of many European peoples. Hallstatt is a place near Salzburg where there were copper and salt mines—ideal if you wanted trade and influence. This center was a natural place for developing the use of the new metal. There are many objects found in other parts of Europe, from Russia to Britain, which are labeled 'Hallstatt': bowls,

Iron tools and weapons, clay pot, and bronze flagon—all from Bronze Age Europe

razors, swords, wagons, pottery, hillforts and the like. Much of the concentration of such objects is in eastern France and Germany. It was among Hallstatt folk of this area that the use of iron spread to the rest of Europe in the period 600–400 B.C. The people concerned were in some cases Celtic speaking, but this does not mean that all Hallstatt culture-users or iron-users were Celts.

The reader must realize that titles like 'Halstatt' are useful terms for grouping cultural features of one period; but an Iron Age warrior in many parts of Europe would have been very startled to be told he was a 'Halstatt warrior'! A similar term used by archeologists is 'La Tène culture', which comes from aspects of an art style of the late 5th century B.C. that are common to La Tène in Switzerland, where finds were made, and many parts of Europe from Scotland to Italy.

One of the most important features of the iron-using cultures of Europe is their contact with the Greek and Roman world.

Hallstatt iron swords

Aspects of the Iron Age in Europe

The words 'Iron Age' are meaningless for many parts of Europe. As with the Bronze Age, such a term rarely indicates a definite date; in fact, many Iron Age peoples sometimes used very little iron, even though some iron may have been smelted in Central Europe as early as 1800 B.C.

In many ways, the most familiar European site in the annals of the Iron Age is Hallstatt in Austria. The Hallstatt cultures of France, Germany, Central and Eastern Europe show evidence of Greek influences.

By the sixth or fifth century B.C., the heyday of Hallstatt was over and the Celts began to make nuisances of themselves all over Europe, even penetrating into Asia Minor. The Celts had a distinctive art of their own but it also owed something to the classical world. The type of site that gave its name to the art and techniques of the period is La Tène in Lake Neuchâtel in Switzerland, where quantities of dintinctively decorated objects were found. This art can loosely be called Celtic. Actually the original 'home'

A place of worship in Iron Age Europe

Celtic art from Britain, France, and Germany

of the La Tène style was in areas near the Rhine.

The cultures of Iron Age peoples throughout Europe include such 'features as the great earth-rampart forts with timber lacings found from Scotland to Germany, as well as the custom of burials with carts, excavated in England, France and Central Europe. Also notable is the use of coins (which were imitations of Greek ones) in the last two centuries B.C., and even the use of a modified alphabet (for some Druids — the Celts' priestly order — kept records).

The hillforts of Britain, the remarkable bronze shields and swords from the Thames, the astonishing gold or bronze collars of the British Iron Age as well as villages like Glastonbury or Little Woodbury, show what a varied culture there was in pre-Roman Britain.

Some Pre-Roman Civilizations of the Mediterranean Area

There is no place here to describe the long-lived culture of the Egyptians that, despite conquerors, survived at least 4,000 years until Caesar's day. Even for the archeologist who is not an Egyptologist, Egyptian finds in Europe have been important in dating Greek and Bronze Age sites.

The Phoenicians, a people of Semitic origin, are credited with introducing writing to the Greeks and subsequently, via the Romans, to the rest of Europe. They were the first navigators to go through the Strait of Gibraltar and are credited with having circumnavigated Africa and reaching the 'Tin Isles' of Cornwall, England. Setting off from cities like Tyre and Sidon (northern Lebanon) they founded great colonies like Carthage. Tyre fell to Alexander in 323 B.C. and Carthage to the Romans in 146 B.C.

Although the Greek heritage to us has been an intellectual one, the archeologist sees the hand of the Greek (or Hellene) in many things: in the municipal architecture of many continents; in the smile and style of a Buddha in a part of India ruled by Greek kings; in the garbled patterns of Iron Age coins in Germany, France and England which had been copied from copies of copies of Greek coins; in the leaf designs of a Greek-influenced Etruscan pot exported to France. Greece (or Hellas) was not so much the present Greece but a spread of settlers and colonies from the Black

Figurines from Cyprus, Spain (Phoenician), and Syria

ships like these,
Greeks carried
r influence
ughout the Mediterranean.

Etruscan wheeled object

Greek vase

Sea and Asia Minor to France and Spain. Sicily and southern Italy were sometimes known as 'Great Greece' because of the number of Greek colonies. The great times of the Greek world, and especially of Athens, were the 8th century B.C. to 133 B.C.

Between 650 and 450 B.C. the Etruscans in central Italy were a powerful people. In some respects, such as their art, they were influenced by the Greeks. For centuries, their well-appointed tombs have been the target of both archeologists and looters.

109

The Romans as an Iron Age People

The Roman world of Scipio, Caesar and Marcus Aurelius has a unity that goes beyond the use of the Latin language. The influence of the Romans in literature, law, and many aspects of life is a cliché of history. But Roman culture, if we include the world and times of Justinian, lasted almost a thousand years and underwent many changes. The archeologist cannot assume that Roman institutions and artifacts remained the same during that time.

First it should be recalled that the Romans who came on the scene and settled in the Alban Hills around the 10th century B.C. were just another early Iron Age (or even late Bronze Age) people. Right to the end of the Roman Empire, the Romans borrowed from the peoples around them—ship designs, weapons, even deities. They were not always the most technologically advanced people; their iron tools and weapons were quite often inferior to those of the barbarians they fought or ruled. Much of the strength of the Romans lay in their capability in organizing and using external elements. In Britain they burned coal; in the Near East they borrowed cavalry techniques; in Rome they learned to wear (and pay for) the costly silks of China; they learned that their strength was in making external peoples *want* to become Romans. At the apex of the Roman Empire, an emperor might be a Spaniard or a Berber or an Arab. Throughout most of its history, Rome learned more from Greece than it ever taught.

It is said that it was in civil engineering and law that the Romans excelled other peoples. Thus it is for their use of concrete, or for their tolerance of the customs of other peoples—customs and laws which they married with their own—that we admire the Romans. While Rome copied much, we must not forget how she indirectly influenced peoples. In Britain same designs on pots show a mingling of Roman and 'Celtic' styles. Roman influence is also seen in the shape of pottery of nations outside the Roman Empire, as in Czechoslovakia.

Roman penetration to those parts was often in the nature of political infiltration, but Roman trade went everywhere.

Left: a Roman hoist, 1st cent. A.D.

Three common Roman pots

Roman soldier

It did not always originate in Rome but went from one part of the empire to another. For example, 'Samian' or 'Terra Sigillata' pots were made in France or western Germany and exported to Britain, Poland, Sweden and elsewhere. Roman trade missions from Syria went to China, and amphorae and Arretine ware from Italy reached India. Isolated Roman objects have even been found in Thailand and Vietnam, but this proves little.

The Roman World

The glorious age of the Roman Empire did not come into being until after the battle of Actium in 31 B.C., but Rome had begun to create an empire with dependent territories centuries before. Thus there were colonies and 'protectorates' long before the times of Caesar and Augustus, and Rome's authority was spread from Spain to Asia Minor. But one should not forget another potent influence on Rome itself. When Rome took over most parts of the Greek-

Hadrian's Wall in Britain

A mosaic, a pot, a coin: three typical artifacts found throughout the Roman world

speaking world in the 2nd century B.C. she was in turn taken over in part by Greek cultures. Besides getting Greek philosophers and writers to come over to teach young Romans, the Romans set Greek technicians and artists to work. Often, therefore, an archeologist may excavate a piece of Greek-influenced art in Africa or Romania (truly a Roman name) or Britain and be faced with sorting out whether it is Roman (most likely) or Greek (not so likely).

The Roman influence on her empire so often merges with that of her subjects that it is hard to distinguish one from the other. A pot found at Meroe (modern Sudan) has a shape that is not Roman, but the slip pattern on it is one that was found in Britain or Germany. Although the Romans had sent a military expedition nearly a thousand miles to Meroe, most Roman objects would have been acquired by peaceable trade.

The Romans were great adaptors of religions, equipment and attire. They got silk from China, and overcoats and baskets from Britain. In return, they helped to provide stability and resistance to the periodic incursions of the barbarians.

Post-Roman migrations

In prehistoric times there were periods of extreme unrest and movement, such as those of around 1200 B.C. and the largely Celtic movements across Europe between 500 and 100 B.C. But few had such a varied impact as the great 'migrations' that took place largely between the second half of the 4th century A.D. and (to close with an arbitrary point of relative quiet) 600 A.D. Generally, food shortages, climatic changes and political vacuums have been suggested as reasons for these shifts of population.

Between 375 and 454 A.D., the fierce Huns rode their way across Eastern and Central Europe. Around the same time, a Germanic people from the areas near the south shores of the Baltic, the Burgundians, began their warlike migrations.

But they were not the only peoples to be on the move. The Goths had left the Baltic areas about the 2nd century A.D. and moved to near the Black Sea. They split and one group, the Visigoths, spread west in the 4th century and defeated the Romans more than once. Beaten by the Franks in 507, the Visigoths finally settled in Spain. The other more Eastern group, the Ostrogoths, mingled their fortunes with the Huns for a time, but finally left Hungary to set up an empire in Italy that lasted from 493 to the 550s when they were defeated by Roman generals from Constantinople.

The Vandals wandered from the Danube lands to Germany. By 409 they, and other peoples, had reached Spain. Twenty years later they crossed the straits to form a North African empire. From Carthage they sacked Rome in 455. They and the other groups mentioned above were a few among many others, such as the Germanic Lombards (6th century) or the Franks from the Rhineland, who rose to power in the 5th and 6th centuries and made themselves into the first stable post-Roman state.

In Britain, the departure of the Romans was followed by Teutonic invasions, first by Celtic peoples and later, in the 5th century A.D., by Jutes, Angles, and Saxons from areas between the mouths of the Rhine and Oder Rivers in Germany.

Much later, Europe was disturbed by one of the last of the vigorous migration peoples, the 'Norsemen' or 'Vikings' who, from the end of the 8th century onward, stirred the world from Iceland to the Holy Land.

Swords, dagger, and brooches
of the post-Roman migrant tribes
of Europe

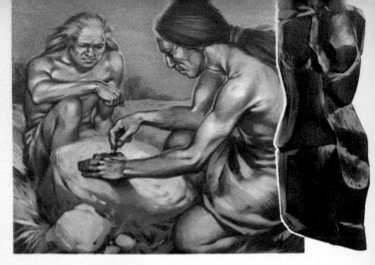

No matter how simple the tools, clothing or
way of life of a people, it all forms a 'culture'
for the archeologist.

Cultures versus Civilizations

The explorer who 'gets back to civilization' (i.e., hot baths,
modern technological aids, etc.) is sure that he is 'civilized'.
Clearly the word 'civilization' is a tricky one, and this is not
helped by the layman's usage when he says, that 'archeologists
look for lost civilizations'.

Most groups of people have a way of life that distinguishes
them entirely or partly from other groups. If 'way of life'
is taken to include all our material possessions, all our mental
and spiritual actions and attitudes, plus our social behavior
and structure, the sum of all this, passed on from generation to
generation, is defined by archeologists as a *culture*. When a
culture of the past is elaborate and powerful, with centralized
control, where there is writing, fine buildings, temples,
monuments, systems of communications or economic
organization such as roads or canals, it is conveniently said
that we have a 'civilization'.

Civilizations cannot begin until after the Neolithic way of

And no matter how old the tools or way
of life of a people—such as these men still hunting
game with bow-and-arrow—archeologists must recognize
the totality of their culture as a 'civilization'.

life has been established, so that an agricultural or cattle-owning system supplies a firm basis for the next important feature in several civilizations: trade.

Civilizations have come and gone. Sometimes they rose for 'obvious' geographical reasons; those of Egypt and Mesopotamia because of the fertility of the Nile, Tigris and Euphrates rivers. Many civilizations fell by conquest, although some decayed internally and crumbled or were nibbled away from outside. Arnold Toynbee's *A Study of History* is one of several valiant attempts to explain the unsolvable problem of the rise and fall of civilizations.

Civilizations can rise independently of each other, as did those of the Old and New Worlds, or they can influence each other, as did those of Greece and Rome. More 'civilizations' in the broadest sense of the term will yet be found in the Neolithic of the Near East and in the Far East; a few more 'civilizations' may be found in Africa and the Americas.

ARCHEOLOGY: PRESENT AND FUTURE

What will the archeologist of the future be like? His training will be more severe in detail and practice and he possibly will not be allowed to specialize in one period too early. Today, the archeologist is an individual; in the future he will be part of a carefully selected team.

It is hoped that the archeologist of the 21st century will have a wider organization to help him: trained workmen, draftsmen, technicians, photographers and recording staff. He should also have a helicopter to survey sites, mobile and stationary laboratories and storage centers for analyzing finds.

With growing understanding of scientific aids, digging will be brisker and more problem-oriented. The information at the digger's fingertips will be prodigious. All archeological literature will have been put into abstract form and stored in a computer memory. A telex message to a record center will answer for him questions like 'At what salt-pan sites, anywhere in the world, have semi-circular support bars of earthenware been found?' Within seconds (and this is no exaggeration) the output printer of a computer at base will print out a list of classified sites and finds. A few minutes later, a photo-printer attached to the apparatus will slide out

Ideally, archeology should have such aids
as this helicopter to function properly.

Equipment is not enough: collaboration is essential.

automatic copies of articles offering parallels to the finds the archeologist has just dug. A sketch of a pot scanned with a phototracer can be made to compare itself automatically with drawings of similar pots in museums elsewhere in the world. Utopian? No, the techniques already exist to carry out the above. But the archeologist cannot do this without paying a personal price. He cannot keep his own index of specialities; he has to share his knowledge quickly. The reward of collaboration will be greater than the personal hoarding.

At the moment, archeology is undergoing a crisis of identity. It uses so many other disciplines that some outsiders have said that it is not a subject in its own right. This is a criticism that has been leveled at geography and other broad disciplines. Yet most people want to know more about mankind's past, and if archeology can cease to borrow uncritically ideas from anthropology, linguistics, sociology, and other subjects, it can become a powerful tool for understanding the growth of man into the future. As digs become more elaborate, they also require much more money.

Archeological Problems and Ethics

The archeologist must not dig just to 'see what's under that mound'. He must be able to prove that he is doing a dig to solve a properly posed problem.

Sometimes the archeologist is called in to do an 'emergency' or 'rescue' dig because a site is threatened. While he is entitled to dig with promptness a site that is going to disappear, it may be that he is doing a dig which could have been anticipated by a well-planned policy.

All excavation is destruction. Many archeologists religiously leave a part of a site, especially a cave, unexcavated so that future workers with superior techniques can return to it later. Another school believes that one can leave too large an area unexcavated, thereby losing valuable clues. There is much to be said for total excavation, but this poses a problem for the conscience: has the excavator the time,

Below: a professional problem-centered dig

storage space, equipment, staff and broad approach that will enable him to write a report on his total excavation?

Quantities of material such as pottery present great problems once excavated. Is the digger to 'select' important pieces without elaborate statistical techniques? What museum can afford the foresight to plan large areas for sorting and warehouses for material waiting to be 'selected'?

At every point, the professional archeologist has to make decisions and exercise judgments that will affect the researchers of the future. His recording, his storage, his relations with other scholars should be close to perfect. The amateur archeologist must not dig for curiosity; he must not maintain private collections that should be in museums; he must be prepared to help recover the archeology of his region even if it is of a period he does not find glamorous.

Below: chaos from poor direction and untrained people

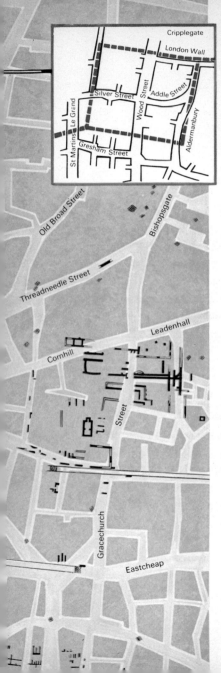

Archeological Prospecting (1)

While it is a matter of ancient faith that the best archeological exploration is done on foot, it is foolish to ignore the help that comes from maps old and new, air photographs and the various methods of geophysical prospecting.

The most modern large-scale maps may reveal ancient roads or settlements, by the way that fields are arranged or by the patterns of areas left uncultivated because they are covered by large stones—but such discoveries made in the library must, of course, be verified on the ground.

Maps that are one or more centuries old may have features on them that are completely buried today and totally unrecognizable on a modern map. However, it is not the antiquity of a map that matters, nor its details, but the interpretation put on it.

For example, the ins-and-outs of the line of the ancient Roman wall in London have long been well-known, but it was not until after World War II that an archeologist

Modern London streets follow the lines of the Roman fort and town.

was able to point out that the northwest corner marked the outline of a Roman military fort that had been built before the walls of London had been erected.

Air photographs, depending on the time of year and day they are taken, can show the archeologist anything from a buried city to a small group of burials. Although air photographs can bring out details of low features because of the shadows at the extremes of a day, most ancient features show up at certain times because of changes in vegetation. A wall buried a little below the surface will make the soil above it shallow, with a corresponding thinning or lighting-up of the grass or vegetation. Similarly, a ditch filled in during the centuries will offer a deeper soil with a corresponding lusher vegetation for the aerial observer to see.

The study of air photographs requires a growing body of techniques nowadays—such as the sophisticated use of stereoscopes and photogrammetric (maps from air photos) equipment,

ng ditches of ancient causewayed mp show in a field.

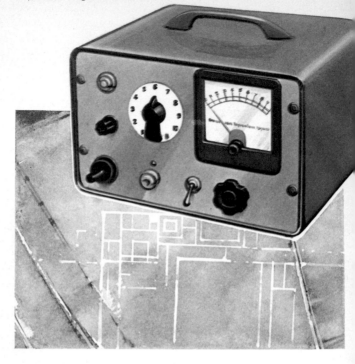

Archeological Prospecting (2)

Since 1945, scientific methods of prospecting in the field have made considerable advances. The main problem is to choose the appropriate apparatus for a particular job. Apparatus can sometimes be costly, but it has been found that small museums or amateur societies have always been able to devise cheaper forms of equipment. There are two main groups of prospecting equipment, although new, radically different types are no doubt being developed as these words are written. The broad groups are (a) the resistivity meters; and (b) magnetometers such as the proton magnetometer and the proton gradiometer.

The resistivity meter is based on the fact that the ground can conduct electricity; different soils or rocks conduct differently. It is clear then the probes linked with a meter placed in the ground will register a certain amount of flow in ordinary earth, but will register differently if a buried wall or filled ditch alters the resistivity of the soil. This kind of apparatus is suited for questions such as: 'Does the wall seen in this excavated area continue below the surface to that end of the field?' Much excavation can be saved if the wall (or a road, or a building) can be picked up farther on.

The magnetometer is a sophisticated apparatus that has been found useful in detecting buried iron, kiln sites, and rubbish pits with certain kinds of soil. The magnetometer detects anomalies or contrasts between the general magnetic field of an area and that above or near a buried object or a kiln several feet below. The instrument is very sensitive and can detect a difference in the field of the ratio 1 to 70,000. Its very sensitivity can be an inconvenience: a large penknife or a bunch of keys in the pockets of a person holding the detector can give a false reading. A car, train or electric power lines too near the equipment can also induce errors.

Surveying with a proton magnetometer

River surveys have proved very useful to the archeologist

Enterprise and Rescue on Land and Water

Many discoveries are made by accident during building operations. Although there are laws in most countries relating to the saving of antiquities, contractors often regard the archeologist as an expensive nuisance who stops work.

An efficient archeologist should be able to anticipate future discoveries from the frequency of past finds in the vicinity. By establishing good public relations with land owners, civil engineers, contractors, agents, public works officials, builders, foremen and workmen, the archeologist can find it easy to persuade them to notice objects and to report them, with the understanding that the archeologist will not create embarrassment for his informants. An archeologist must not break trust after an agreement is made; once he breaks faith informants may become as silent as clams. As in the world of spy fiction, the rescue-archeologist, even though he may be an

126

official, sometimes has to make 'deals' which might appear reprehensible officially and academically, for the sake of winning future knowledge. Sometimes he has to forego access to one site to win access to many other sites.

In recent years, one form of archeology that has come to play an increasingly important role is underwater archeology, but to the serious scholar it can be both a delight and a source of distress. From the findings of gold ritual objects in the great sacred well at Chichen Itza in Yucatan, Mexico, to the raising of the 17th-century ship *Vasa* off Sweden, underwater archeology has excited the world. Shiploads of ancient goods have been found: a scattered cargo of Roman 'Samian' ware off the coast of Kent, or a Bronze Age vessel loaded with ingots, scrap and implements of about 1200 B.C. found off Cape Gelidonya, Turkey. Groups of contemporary objects such as are found in a ship's hold are invaluable as dating evidence.

But time and time again objects have been taken irrevocably out of context by divers archeologically inexperienced or archeologists with inadequate underwater experience.

The archeologist often needs the goodwill of 'locals' to track down sites.

The Hunt for Clues

No archeologist will have time to walk over every corner of his 'territory'. Even if he has maps, air photographs and good local contacts he cannot spot everything himself. What clues must he teach himself and his informants to use? No example of any clue will apply to every part of the world. In temperate countries, the nettle *(Urtica dioica)* seen in a lonely spot may indicate past human occupation. A ring of nettles in a field might show the presence of the filled ditch of a burial barrow. In the United States, sage *(Salvia subincisa)* has turned up, significantly, at pre-Colombian ruin sites.

But botanical clues are just a few among a thousand possible clues. A British archeologist sees Norse place-names in Lancashire and tries to follow up the Viking history of the area. In Spain, archeologists note that one region has a concentration of Celtic place-names. Conclusions about early Celtic settlements can then be made, especially if there are excavated finds of the 8th century B.C. that confirm the presence of such settlers.

Sometimes a distribution map may show up connections

Place-names often give clues of prehistoric settlements
—as do these Celtic sites in France, Spain and Portugal.

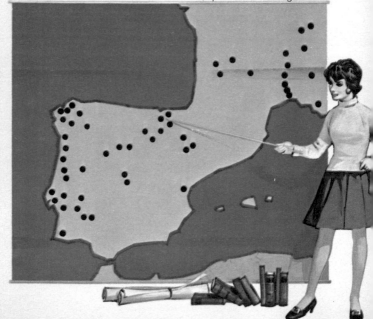

Certain plants offer clues about past settlements.

that are not clear on the ground, but there are perils. An archeologist finds that there are upright stone monuments at many places where Neolithic polished stone axes are found. In fact the coincidence is too good to be true. The standing stones may be of the Late Migration period or as late as the 10th century A.D. They are placed near settlements where soil was good, and this is where Neolithic man had been — three thousand years before.

One of the best examples of the good use of clues comes from the story of archeological researches in India and Pakistan. Before the coming of radiocarbon dating, dating was difficult. A systematic survey was undertaken in many museums for *Roman* pots found at sites in the Indian subcontinent. Eventually a few were found, and the places where they were most plentiful were excavated until a layer was found with Roman pottery shards in it. The layers above and below it were then fixed relative to Roman times, and a workable chronology began to be forged.

Survey and Recording

The archeologist, whether professional or amateur, has to learn the art of plotting finds and making plans of sites and digs. While he does not have to be a professional surveyor or mathematician, he must be familiar with the basic techniques of using survey tapes or chains, the surveying prismatic compass, the level and the theodolite. In some terrains he will need to be able to use a plane-table.

Before he begins an excavation, or immediately after he has discovered a new site, the archeologist must be able to carry out speedy surveys which can readily be transferred to paper or onto map plans. He has to have the judgment that chooses the correct standard of accuracy—it is no use measuring a wall-thickness to the nearest millimeter, if the drawn wall will be a thinly marked hair-line on a map.

The *level* is used for checking trench levels and relating a site and its layers to a standard datum level; it is essential for contours or for checking whether one end of a structure or level has subsided. Environmental archeologists find the level invaluable for relating sites to ancient river terraces or shorelines.

The large surveying prismatic compass or the more accurate theodolite are the best instruments for preparing the ground plan of an excavation area or a group of structures. The theory of these instruments is easy to learn, but constant practice will be needed to ensure ease of handling. Such instruments will help on a survey to detect deviations from a right-angle of buildings or to fix a newly discovered site in relation to known landmarks. If properly calibrated, the telescope of a theodolite will find the distance of a survey staff from the instrument.

The plane-table is at its best in large tracts of treeless country. The main landmarks in a thousand square miles can be plotted in an afternoon. There are several ways of using a plane-table and old methods may still suit modern sites.

In the next decade, new types of apparatus will make surveying even more automatic for the archeologist.

Right, above: a surveyor's prismatic compass
Right, below: leveling with a staff

Excavation: The Basic Kit

Archeological tools must be as varied as the many tasks that are required in an excavation. For delicate work such as digging a skeleton, a small brush and the slenderest of dental probes seem almost crude. At other times, a bulldozer to remove 19th-century urban rubble is essential. Sometimes a pick or a shovel can be used safely, but in most layers the smallest scraping tool is best. In many countries, the brick-layer's pointed trowel is the preferred tool.

The excavated and sifted soil must be removed promptly, whether by manual labor or by a conveyer to a spoil heap which is conveniently near and yet not too near for danger. Elaborate safety precautions must be taken to prevent collapse.

The greater the variety of an archeologist's equipment the better

- ~~hangers~~
- ~~dishtowel~~ + asst washcloth
- movie projector
- ~~you~~
- ~~big clean chair~~
- ~~night books~~ | handball glove
- armory + bowstring
- Stapler
- kids picture frames
- ~~basket~~ ~~clock~~ +
- ~~kids bath little thing~~
- ~~baby snoop Susan~~
- ~~bikini~~ globe lamp
- ~~slinger~~
- ~~foot bath~~ + ~~swings~~
- negligee, night lite
- punch bowl
- patio table
- bowstring, target

Evans sina 64

conservation lab work
prevent decomposition
study disciplines:
geol. soil science
chemistry biology
palentology history
philology physical
anthro cultural
anthro statistics
computer science
surveying mapping
photography

Glyn Daniel British archaeologist
worth reading

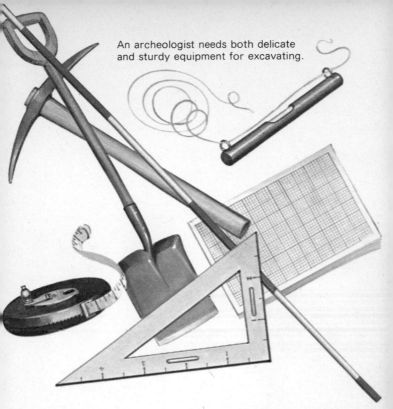

An archeologist needs both delicate and sturdy equipment for excavating.

An efficient excavation has a variety of ingenious apparatus available: photographic towers, pumps, concrete breakers for urban sites, ladders and so on. Some excavators in rainy climates use giant plastic canopies. Obviously it is not possible to learn from books what is essential equipment.

In many countries there are excavations which are run by local societies that have competent excavators but may be handicapped by inadequate equipment. Each kind of excavation needs special equipment and this may require maintenance and repair during the months before the dig starts. Anticipation of even minor details is vital. Is there fencing adequate to deal with both children and animals? The means to cope with mud? Does the toolshed have an adequate padlock?

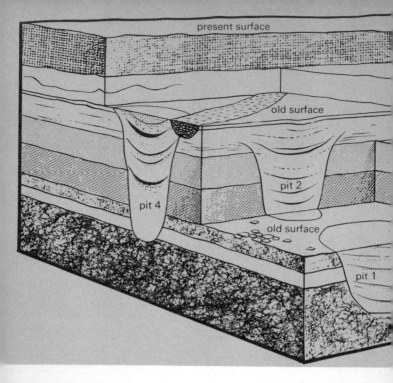

present surface

old surface

pit 2

pit 4

old surface

pit 1

Excavation: Layers

It is not the depth above sea level at which an object was found that matters. The important thing is to know in what layer something was found and, in addition, how and when the layer was deposited. This means that the finding of objects can, paradoxically, be less important than interpreting a layer. What good is it to find an artistic object and to keep such poor records of the site that you cannot assign it with certainty to a Roman or a Bronze Age layer?

There are a thousand practicalities involved in the excavation of a site. No book can teach the skillful movement of a scraping tool that, in the hands of the digger, senses that a change in soil texture heralds the revealing of a new layer. No manual can adequately describe the techniques by which every detail of the layers is recorded interpretatively. It is

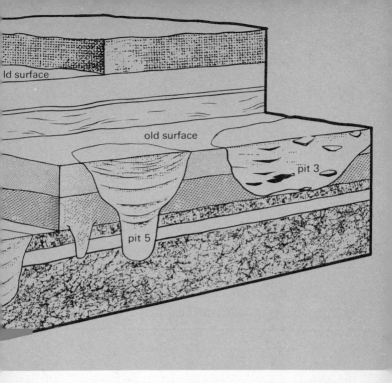

old surface

old surface

pit 3

pit 5

The layers in an excavation can often be more complicated than this.

better to record how a layer lies and supply some knowledge of how it was formed than to describe its coloration in artistic detail. Nevertheless, a sharp eye must be kept on a layer at several stages of an excavation. At first it may be moist and sticky. A few days later it is a little dusty. Judicious scraping when the section is being drawn may reveal traces of charcoal or a general slope. Dense rootlet patterns may indicate where there once had been timber.

The excavator must draw all the layers, having numbered them physically with labels. The drawing should have all the layers numbered and, where possible, enough symbols or captions should go with the section-drawing to assist the reader and enable him to grasp the full significance of all the layers.

Equipment for Recording or Packaging

Good excavation needs good recording. Meticulousness in recording is essential, since a new find is so obvious to the eye that it seems unbelievable that in a few months people who were present will disagree violently as to which way up it lay.

Essentials for an excavation include:

(a) Large notebook—a log of activities, with sketches in it.
(b) Layer labels (for marking excavated layers).
(c) Two labels similar to (b) to go with finds.
(d) Photographs. These must be documented serially or they are useless.
(e) Drawing board and good-quality paper.
(f) Bags, boxes and crates: all to be well-labeled.
(g) Marking of finds (best done in India ink or paints). If labels are used they must be firmly fixed.
(h) Numbering of finds: *e.g.*, AB1969/3834, which means

this is item 3834 of a series dug in 1969 at a site coded as 'AB'. There are many variants of this method.

(i) Finds record book. Each item must have the source site area, layer, position, etc. listed. Leave blank columns for comments or sketches. Note that some excavators prefer to use cards instead.

Make sure that jars, specimen tubes, etc. have indelible labels inside as well as outside.

An excavator should do what he can to have containers and packaging suitable for all eventualities. Some finds must be kept moist on their way to a conservation laboratory; other items like shards should be dry before they are put into storage. Soils and many organic substances grow fungus quickly if incorrectly packed. Flints, prehistoric shards and, indeed, all finds should be packed so that they do not rub or grate when traveling.

Left: a consistent system must be used to mark pots, labels, boxes, etc.
Below: recording equipment must be the best.

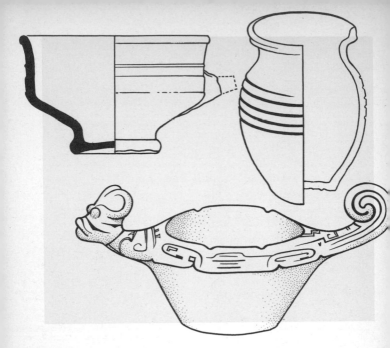

Some U.S. and European conventions for drawing pots

Some Archeological Drawing Conventions

When objects are dug up, it is often important to get good photographs made of them. Properly taken photographs with scales, good lighting and the use of appropriate lenses and film are invaluable as records. But photographs are expensive and often a drawing in India ink will be more useful for comparisons than a photograph.

Special conventions have been devised for showing objects and their key dimensions. It is not likely that the conventions will become international, but each archeologist tries to be consistent with his own practice and those of his colleagues in his own field.

Pots are usually shown 'half x-rayed'. Texture is only shown in special cases. Flint tools are shown with flake hollows indicated by inked lines; other stone implements are often shown by stippling. Badly corroded metal can also be shown by stippling since there is rarely any chance of confusion. Smooth metal is often rendered by a minimum of parallel hatchings.

There are many conventions for showing ground features like ditches or rising ground. These can be observed from the published practice of the best archeologists in various countries; in all cases, the convention that uses the least amount of ink is the most desirable.

All drawings, whether of Iron Age forts or Bronze Age pins, should show cross-sections. A cross-section can be of diagnostic importance; it should not be assumed that the reader can guess at it. In addition, there should be neat captions and labels on the drawings so that they become self-explanatory. The reader should not be forced to flip back and forward among pages to get explanations of drawings.

Last but not least, there should be a scale, preferably a linear scale rather than the statement 'all objects 1:2' or worse, 'scales 1:2 to 1:5'. All drawings in a report should, if possible, be numbered in an order that matches the sequence of the text.

Leather and metalwork illustrated with archeologists' conventions

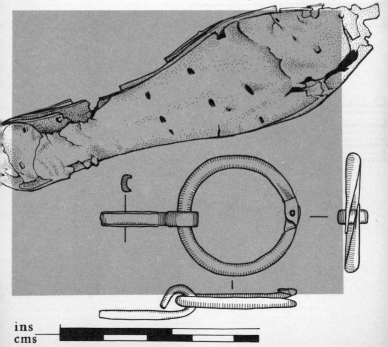

Archeologists learn about the environment of a culture from finds such as these seeds from a prehistoric site in Germany.

Detective Work

The systematic excavator cannot depend only on obvious finds such as pottery, tools, art objects and the like. He has to study *context* with the diligence that a detective brings to bear on a crime. Once, in the Neolithic period, for example, a newly made pot was put on the ground, and from this we know that the maker ate barley. The clue came from the shapes of grain picked up by the pot. The grains were burnt away during the firing, but the identifiable hollow survived.

A piece of something gray, sticky and indefinable is dug up: the trained excavator must have the ability or equipment to make a preliminary assessment, plus knowing what experts to consult. The object might be wax, or butter, or fish-waste from a mound of shells, or even a part of a human body preserved in an acidic soil!

The ancient *environment* represented by an excavated layer represents a major part of an archeologist's task. From insect and animal remains and pollen types that indicate ancient vegetation, he can learn about the climate of the time.

All detective work has to be done with an awareness that things can go wrong. For example, samples of burnt wood or other carbon sources can contain minute amounts of 'carbon-14', the proportion of which indicates how long ago it was since the wood was 'alive'. This method can sometimes date organic matter up to about 30,000 years old, but contamination by older or younger carbon will throw the dating off.

The scientist uses techniques every day that may be of use to the archeologist, if the latter takes the trouble of learning some science. For example, bones buried in the ground take up, over time, small quantities of the element fluorine. Two bones buried at the same time in the same place should contain the same amount of fluorine; a bone introduced next to another that has been there a long time already will have less fluorine. This method of relative chronology is useful in detecting the faking of evidence (as for the Piltdown finds) or for checking whether a bone found in gravel is older than another lying with it.

Upper: testing in a radiocarbon dating lab. Below: amount of fluorine (blue columns) increases with time bones have remained buried.

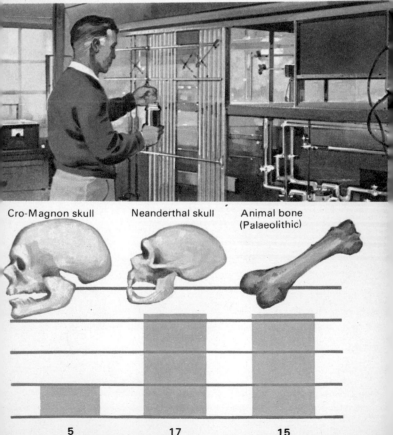

Cro-Magnon skull   Neanderthal skull   Animal bone (Palaeolithic)

5   17   15

Dating by Annual Layers

Each year new methods of dating objects and deposits are optimistically announced. These approaches are so varied and require such elaborate apparatus and know-how that here it is better to discuss only two techniques that have been used with reasonable success during the last 50 years: *tree-ring dating* and *varve chronology*.

Trees should produce a new ring each year. For various reasons (which are modified by climate, soil and the tree species) the rings vary in thickness. In a particular species of tree grown in one area, there will be found a sequence of combinations of thick and thin rings that can be similar for trees of the same date, e.g., thick, thin, thick, thick, thin, thin. Let us describe this simply as $+-++--$ and consider a recently cut stump that has, outward from the center, this sequence for the *first* eighteen years of its life: $+----$ $-++++----+---$ . . . and so on to the bark of this tree, which is 200 years old. If nearby a roughly hewn beam is excavated or a barn timber is noted which has at one corner the sequence $+----+++ +----+---$ and bark fragments, we can see that the similarity is exact and that the log was cut some 200 years ago. Subsequent finds of older beams will produce overlapping sequences which will help provide a dating sequence. Tree-ring dating has been

Tree rings have helped to
date the wood used in
an old Russian town.

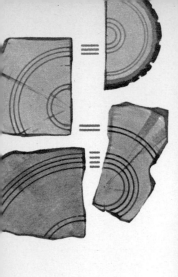

Above: overlapping sequences in different wood
samples help provide a long time sequence.
Right: counting varves laid down in an
old lake bed.

used to date the sequence of log streets in medieval Novgo-
rod in the U.S.S.R. and to date American Indian sites that
go back 2,000 years.

Varve dating depends on the turbulent spring waters that
come down from glaciated areas; they deposit, at first, rough
material in lakes but later, in the autumn, drop only the
finest silt until all deposition stops in the winter. Each year
a layer, or *varve*, is added. Varves vary in thickness and offer
sequences that vary sufficiently to be analyzed like tree-
rings. In certain lake-deposits of Scandinavia and North
America it has been possible to count back (often using
strings of adjacent lakes for overlaps) either to some year
dated by a special inundation or right back to the period
immediately after the last retreat of the glaciers.

Among the problems connected with tree-ring and varve
counting is that is some years no new ring or layer is produced; occasionally a tree can produce two rings in a season,
or a lake two or more varves in a year.

143

Conservation and Restoration

Objects buried in the ground often reach an equilibrium with their environment. The rate of decay is then at a minimum. If the object is organic, it is saved from decomposition by a constant moisture content which may retain soil chemicals that help preservation. Once the object is excavated, it is liable to lose water and to be affected by night and day temperature changes: decomposition then often proceeds fast. Fungi and bacteria find excavated items irresistible. Preservation or conservation of an object will depend on speedy handling by a trained specialist. Careful wrapping to retain moisture may be of some use, but with inexpert wrapping the object becomes a focal point for mold growth.

During the speedy and complex assessment of the condition of a find, the archeologist-conservator must consider the nature of the soil. An acid site, such as a peat bog, will soften the bones of a burial but preserve the flesh; an alkaline deposit, such as chalk, will keep only the bones intact.

Many organic substances like leather, wood and cloth are restored by impregnation with chemical substances that replace the moisture-filling of cavities. Metals, especially iron and lead, are extremely difficult to preserve from further

breakdown. Again, what seems to be a copper or bronze coin may be basically a silver one; the copper has 'migrated' to the outside and poses a problem. Sometimes the corrosion products are removed by tools and sometimes by electrolysis. Preliminary x-ray of metal is recommended since even the most skillful cleaning may lose features such as inlays. An x-ray photograph will detect the patterns in the original metal even if every part of it is rust or verdigris.

Conservation to prevent deterioration is just one problem. Other problems arise, since an object has to be made feasible for museum display or for study. This can be very difficult. Pots can be restored with plastic fibers or plaster and painted, but there is a sort of 'ethic' that prevents the part mended from looking too much like the original. Otherwise one might draw false conclusions about the pot's condition.

Writing-up and Records

The archeologist who has excavated a site has *destroyed* evidence. What he has dug cannot be put back for reconsideration. Having dug he must publish, however unspectacular the results are. If no publisher or periodical can

A modern laboratory for conserving archeological finds

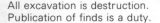

All excavation is destruction.
Publication of finds is a duty.

find space for the results of a dig, the archeologist should at least deposit a copy of his report and drawings in the regional museum. Printing costs are high nowadays, but many archeologists are willing to forego the dignity of print and make their finds known in duplicated or mimeographed form.

A published report should have a short synopsis at the beginning or end. The report should be brief but not too cryptic or allusive. Most archeological reports will be read in countries outside that of its origin, so the author has to be careful even when writing about what seems obvious: there is a Santiago in Spain, one in Chile, one in Argentina, as well as one in Cuba. The county or province or district an archeologist works in may gain in fame from such writings — as long as he mentions where it is. A good report will have key maps showing precisely where a site is.

A report should have illustrations of key objects drawn with enough systematic care to make them comparable with similar objects found in museums or other illustrations. However, an accurate scale must be included so that the

146

reader will be able to see exactly what size an object is.

Throughout his report, the archeologist supplies parallels from both similar and dissimilar cultures. Everything is written to help the reader, whether he is a professional or a member of the public. Usually a bibliography goes at the end of the article, as do special topics such as the museums where the finds are kept and the list of acknowledgments of help. Modern archeology reports often contain appendices by such specialists as botanists, zoologists, geologists, metallurgists, textile experts, etc. They should be skillfully cross-linked with the main text.

There are many other ways of collecting and disseminating archeological facts: card index systems describing finds or sites, kept not by individuals but in museums or universities or the headquarters of societies, are invaluable. Another useful thing is a system of promptly published short abstracts on all archeological articles produced in one country, enabling an archeologist to get a bird's eye view of current work.

Systematic drawings (with scales) and information retrieval techniques are essential for modern archeological research.

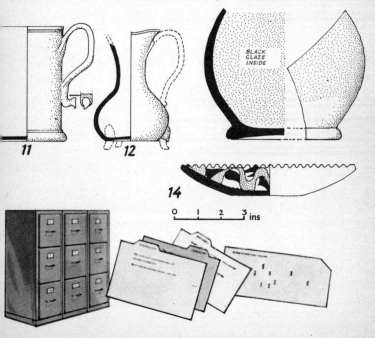

Archeological Societies

With the growth of archeology in many countries, the amateur can increase his chances of becoming an effective part-time worker. He must, of course, persuade professionals and archeological officialdom that he is neither a crank nor a dilettante. Despite increased state control—which is intended to check both philistinism and treasure hunters—the amateur has made himself increasingly useful and furthered archeological enquiry.

The volunteer has to impress by his diligence and initiative in *observing* and *recording*. This requires a background of reading and museum visits that should be enhanced by membership in a reputable archeological society. A well-run local society is a stimulus to study and a valuable aid to official archeology.

First, a society should see to the *training* of its members by organizing lectures, classes and outings. More experienced members and friendly professionals should

Good training and field work are requisites of amateur archeologist

do all they can to raise standards, thus benefiting archeology as a whole.

Practical work is important but there should not be a childish haste to excavate. Many other useful activities besides digging come under the banner of archeology: clearing vegetation from ancient sites, restoring old walls or archaic industrial structures, and plotting or photographing antiquities and old buildings.

The archeological 'health' of a country is to be measured by the efficiency and standards of local societies. A handful of renowned and brilliant specialists in high places is not enough.

The running of a society can be reduced to a formalized structure. But officers have to be good sociologists and psychologists. Extraordinary things go on: scapegoats occur, small groups hog activities and we have what is politely called the 'clash of personalities'. Such unpleasant facts are, unfortunately, as much a part of archeology as the rain that stops a dig or a collapse of soil on diggers.

Although amateurs deserve credit for making valuable discoveries, they must know when to turn the major excavating over to professionals.

149

The Museum

Fortunately few people nowadays see museums as dreary or dusty places. But many do not realize that a good museum should be like the proverbial iceberg: most of the mass below the surface. If everything is on show, the visitor tires in eye and spirit. Thus a good museum might display as little as one percent of its total collections. Exhibits will be chosen for their beauty, or as local types or as dating specimens. Displays should be changed at not too long intervals.

A museum has to be a depository for much material that would be lost or unrecognized by untrained people, but scholars and the serious amateur will want access to the reference collections of a museum. So special cases, storerooms, or galleries are needed. Often the real reputation of a museum hinges on the efficiency of its backroom storage and catalogues.

A museum must not be a warehouse of unwanted things. It should be the home of systematically collected samples of man's culture. A museum is not just for scholars; all society can benefit from it. For example, a textile designer can find ancient motifs for modern patterns; a film director can get authentic background for a period film; a young production engineer sees how basic techniques and basic prejudices can guide or hinder progress. Most important of all, the child learns in the museums to love history as a subject.

In the past, people regarded a museum as a storage box into which one might respectfully peep. Today a curator can visualize his museum as a lens—or, if you like, a television screen—in which the past becomes not merely vivid but relevant. From seeing change in the past, we are made to focus on change in the present and the future.

Well-run museums need not depend so much on eminent curators as on an enthusiastic staff. Without a conservation officer and a staff of archeological explorers and folk-life specialists, a museum becomes a sluggish tortoise. These, in turn, depend on technicians, photographers, display artists, carpenters, painters, cleaners, security men, sales staff (visitors like to buy postcards, booklets, and replicas) and many others. Up-to-date museums have a large staff of specialists who concentrate their attention on dealing with the interests of schools and children.

A good museum should have storerooms organized in
great detail (above) but its displays (below) should
be simplified.

151

Kinds of Archeology

People who make archeology the great interest of their lives can be too specialized in their tastes. Interest in Egyptology, the Romans or the Maya can swamp and paralyze curiosity about other periods and people. While it is wise to concentrate on certain topics, it is foolish to do so to the extent that one is incapable of being interested about other aspects of archeology. There are not enough archeologists, and there are too many regions needing well-rounded workers for developing a policy of research and exploration.

Prehistory deals with the story of man or of peoples that lived before they possessed writings and records. Prehistoric peoples left no writings and inscriptions; all we can learn about them is by the detective methods of the archeologist. Occasionally prehistoric peoples who had no writing are mentioned by the Greeks or Romans or the Egyptians. One

Examples of the variety of evidence that archeologists must be prepared to deal with include an Australian limekiln, medieval mason marks, and an Inca wall.

Archeologists may learn from such things as (left) a restored 15th-century house in Wales; (right above) comparing changes in fashions; and (below) Viking brooches.

can have a battle, for example, between the historical Marius or Caesar and a 'prehistoric' Celtic people, but the general concept of prehistory is clear.

Some prehistorians may enjoy a spell working on the archeology of historical peoples. There is a satisfaction in linking a Chinese bronze to a particular dynasty or a piece of Amerindian pottery with a specific pueblo culture. There has also arisen a concern for industrial archeology: this is not merely the study of the material remains of the Industrial Revolution, but can be systematic research into development of trades, technology and production of all ages and lands. In the United States, colonial and Civil War archeology is a very active field—witness the many on-site reconstructions of houses and other buildings that have been made all over the country. Williamsburg is a well-known example.

A good archeologist will try to spread his interests widely to get the stimuli that always come from meeting people working in adjoining fields of study.

153

A SELF-TESTING QUIZ

Some of the objects below can be identified from pictures earlier in the book. A few items are of a new type; they are introduced to help you think about unknown objects. The answers are printed upside down on p. 155.

14

15

16

18

17

Answers

1. Skull of *Homo sapiens neanderthalensis*, France
2. Carved figure from late Mesolithic village in Yugoslavia
3. Plastered skull from pre-pottery Neolithic, Jericho
4. Neolithic pot, China
5. Neolithic pot, England
6. Greek amphora, Athens, 86 B.C.
7. Flint dagger of Beaker period, found in the Thames River in London
8. Beaker, late Neolithic, from England
9. Clovis point from the United States, c. 9000 B.C.
10. Folsom point from the United States, c. 8000 B.C.
11. Mousterian scraper, France
12. Geometric Mesolithic flints, France
13. Handax, France, Paleolithic
14. Knight, 12th century, on tapestry, Norway
15. Roman milestone from England, 120-121 A.D.
16. Engraved pebble, Upper Paleolithic, France: a hairy mammoth
17. Norse-type sword found in U.S.S.R., 11th century A.D.
18. Bronze Age rapier, England, c. 1000 B.C.

BOOKS TO READ

No single list could include all the books on archeology in all its aspects, so we offer here a selection of books that introduce the general public to some of the fundamentals of modern approaches to archeology.

Teach Yourself Archaeology. S. Graham Birks. Roy.

World Prehistory. Grahame Clark. Cambridge.

Origins and Growth of Archaeology. Glyn Daniel. Crowell.

Ships, Shoals and Amphoras: The Story of Underwater Archaeology. Suzanne DeBorhegyi. Holt.

Invitation to Archaeology. James Deetz. Doubleday.

Archaeological Techniques for Amateurs. Philip C. Hammond. Van Nostrand.

Introduction to Prehistoric Archeology. Frank Hole and R. F. Heizer. Holt.

Approach to Archeology. Stuart Piggott. McGraw-Hill.

Scientist and Archaeologist. Ed. by Edward Pyddoke. Roy

Amateur Archaeologist's Handbook. Maurice Robbins and M. B. Irving. Crowell.

Frontiers in Archeology. Robert Silverberg. Chilton.

Archaeology From the Earth. Robert E. M. Wheeler. Penguin.

MUSEUMS TO VISIT

The best 'museums' are the actual excavations; aside from these, many fine collections bring archeology alive. So many, in fact, that we have had to omit from our list certain types that anyone should be able to find in literally every state: collections of local and regional archeology; collections of American Indian cultures; and university and college museums, both public and private. Canadians, by the way, have their National Museum in Ottawa and the Royal Ontario Museum in Toronto, while Mexico has its National Archeological Museum in Mexico City.

Alabama: Birmingham Museum of Art. *Arizona:* Phoenix: The Heard Museum of Anthropology. *California:* Berkeley: Pacific School of Religion Archaeology Museum; Los Angeles: County Museum of History and Science. *Colorado:* Denver Museum of Natural History. *District of Columbia:* Smithsonian Institution. *Georgia:* Augusta Museum. *Hawaii:* Honolulu: Bishop Museum and Academy of Arts. *Illinois:* Chicago Natural History Museum. *Louisiana:* New Orleans: Delgado Museum of Art. *Maryland:* Baltimore: Walters Art Gallery. *Massachusetts:* Boston Museum of Fine Arts; Cambridge: Peabody Museum. *New York:* American Museum of Natural History; Brooklyn Museum; Metropolitan Museum of Art. *Ohio:* Akron Art Institute; Cincinnati Art Museum; Cleveland Museum of Art. *Pennsylvania:* Pittsburgh: Carnegie Institute Museum. *Texas:* Houston Museum of Fine Arts.

INDEX

Add to your
KNOWLEDGE
THROUGH
COLOR

(All Books $1.45 Each)
(Where marked ⓢ $1.95 Each)

The opposite page lists the currently available and constantly growing books in this new paperback series. To add to your KNOWLEDGE THROUGH COLOR library simply list the titles and mail to:

BANTAM BOOKS, INC.
Dept. KTC-1
666 Fifth Avenue
New York, N.Y. 10019

Add 25¢ to your order to cover postage and handling. Send check or money order — please! We cannot be responsible for orders containing cash.

— A Free Bantam Catalog Available Upon Request —